Advance praise for *M...*
by Ariell...

"*Magical Souvenirs* is a tribute to the mystical miracles that can happen when we leave the safety of what is known and travel to exotic places in the world and in our own hearts."
—Judith Orloff, M.D.,
author of *Dr. Judith Orloff's Guide to Intuitive Healing* and *Second Sight*

"Traveling can be a most delightful way to open yourself up to new experiences of personal transformation. Whether you are looking for a miracle or divine guidance or simply a deeper understanding of yourself, the stories in *Magical Souvenirs* will inspire you to travel to the deepest parts of your heart and soul as well as exotic lands around the world."
—Debbie Ford,
author of *The Dark Side of the Light Chasers*

Praise for Arielle Ford's
Hot Chocolate for the Mystical Soul series

"These remarkable stories will challenge your beliefs, stretch your mind, open your heart, and expand your consciousness."
—Jack Canfield, author of *Chicken Soup for the Soul*

"It's better than hot chocolate because it has no calories. It definitely makes your insides warm."
—Marianne Williamson,
author of *Healing the Soul of America*

ARIELLE FORD is the author of the *Hot Chocolate for the Mystical Soul* series (available from Plume), and the president of the Ford Group, a public relations firm whose clients have included Deepak Chopra, Neale Donald Walsch, Marianne Williamson, Gary Zukav, Dean Ornish, Jack Canfield, and Mark Victor Hansen. She lives in La Jolla, California, with her husband, Brian.

"A wonderful way to get in touch with the deepest meanings and the grandest messages of life . . . These stories touch the heart of the human experience."

—Neale Donald Walsch

"Stories that enthrall and stimulate us . . . Bound to change forever the way we perceive the world."

—Deepak Chopra

"This book has an amazing collection of magical and mystical stories. I highly recommend it for anyone who is fascinated with the spiritual realm of life."

—Marci Shimoff, co-author, *Chicken Soup for the Woman's Soul*

"A magical collection of heartwarming human stories that inspire us to find goodness and spirituality in our lives."

—Judith Orloff, M.D., author of *Second Sight*

"Every page invites you to a more perfect connection to your soul. Beautifully done."

—Wayne Dyer, author of *Manifest Your Destiny*

MAGICAL SOUVENIRS

★

True Spiritual Adventures
from Around the World

ARIELLE FORD

A PLUME BOOK

PLUME
Published by the Penguin Group
Penguin Putnam Inc., 375 Hudson Street,
New York, New York 10014, U.S.A.
Penguin Books Ltd, 80 Strand,
London WC2R 0RL, England
Penguin Books Australia Ltd, Ringwood,
Victoria, Australia
Penguin Books Canada Ltd, 10 Alcorn Avenue,
Toronto, Ontario, Canada M4V 3B2
Penguin Books (N.Z.) Ltd, 182–190 Wairau Road,
Auckland 10, New Zealand

Penguin Books Ltd, Registered Offices:
Harmondsworth, Middlesex, England

First published by Plume,
a member of Penguin Putnam Inc.

First Printing, March 2002
10 9 8 7 6 5 4 3 2 1

Grateful acknowledgment is made for permission to reprint the following: "The Mystery of Lost Time" by Gregg Braden, an excerpt from *The Isaiah Effect* by Gregg Braden. Copyright © 2000 by Gregg Braden. Reprinted by permission of Harmony Books, a division of Random House, Inc. "Sahara: The Fruitful Void" by Roger Housden, adapted and expanded with permission of Roger Housden and Simon & Schuster from *Sacred Journeys in a Modern World* by Roger Housden. Copyright © 1998 by Roger Housden.

 REGISTERED TRADEMARK—MARCA REGISTRADA

CIP data is available.
ISBN 0-452-28305-1

Printed in the United States of America
Set in Sabon
Designed by Eve Kirch

For Aunt Pearl
whose tales of trips abroad sparked my love of travel

Contents

Acknowledgments xiii

Introduction xv

I. The Unexplainable

Prison Breakout, *Maggie L. Cooper* 3

The Mystery of Lost Time, *Gregg Braden* 5

The Great White Shark, *Jeremiah Sullivan* 8

Greek Ghosts, *Stephanie Gunning* 12

Bouncing Stones, *Kerry Louise Atlee* 14

Gateway to Another Dimension, *Triana Jackie Hill* 16

Finding Peace in Taos, *Pam Brown* 21

The Mountain Miracle, *Deardra Shuler* 24

A Mystery in Arabic, *Mike G. Doty* 26

Journey, *Micki East, M.A.* 28

Wiltshire Crop Circle, *Victoria Bullis* 31

II. Sacred Sites, Synchronicity, and Shamanism

Aliki's Miracle, *Constantin M. Caradimitropoulo* 37

The Storyteller in Kadita, *Jessie Heller-Frank* 39

Dreamer, *Renu Dudani* 43

A Merseyside Miracle, *Kathleen McGowan* 46

The Gods Look Down, *Rik Cooke* 49

Sicilian Synchronicities, *Rosanne M. Siino* 52

Butterfly Magic and the Moody Blues, *Alan Moore*   55
Journey by Water, *Stephanie Gunning*   59
The Mysterious Mayan Shaman, *Jill V. Mangino*   64
The Wrong Pub at the Right Time, *Kathleen McGowan*   68
The Wake-Up Call, *Donna LeBlanc, M.Ed., D.A.P.A.*   72
Baba Bakala: A Glimpse of the Divine,
   Dharma Singh Khalsa, M.D.   77
My Soul Retrieval, *Irina H. Corten, Ph.D.*   81
Medugorje Materialization, *Iris Freelander, D.D.*   86
I Will Never Forget, *Elizabeth Seely*   89

III. DREAMS AND VISIONS

Gifts of the Goddesses, *Arielle Ford*   95
A Visit to the Heavenly Kitchen, *Sarabeth Archer*   97
The First Time I Saw the Angels, *Connie Kaplan*   103
Journey Through the Keening Space, *Leslie Lynne*   107
Time Travel, *Julie Isaac*   110
Spiritual Awakenings, *Mark Gonzaga*   114
Dreamtime Dharma, *Jeremiah Abrams*   118
10,000 Buddhas, *Frances Heussenstamm, Ph.D.*   123
At the Sign of Three Crosses, *Peggy J. Cain*   125
The Eagle's Gift, *Josie RavenWing*   129

IV. PROPHECY AND OMENS

The Fortune-Telling Birds of Hong Kong, *Arielle Ford*   135
Thank You, Sai Baba, *James F. Twyman*   138
Conversations with a Bird, *Jill Lublin*   142
Through My Father's Eyes, *Gail Albert*   146
Deepak's Mushroom Omelette, *Arielle Ford*   149
Matchmakers in Heaven, *Lora Vivas*   153
Remember Today, *Roger W. Clevenger*   155

V. DIVINE INTERVENTION: HEALING, PRAYER, AND MEDITATION

Sidling Hill, *Nancy E. Myer*   159
Angel with a Lantern, *Jill H. Lawrence*   165
Popocatépetl, *Donald D. Hartman*   170
Message from My Mother, *Kathleen Keith*   178
Amazing Grace, *Lacey Hawk*   181
Moment in Midair, *Judith Wright*   184
Sahara: The Fruitful Void, *Roger Housden*   188
A Farmer's Advice, *George R. Noory*   193
Saved by a Voice, *George Wrigley*   194
Lessons in English, *Mary Lennon*   196
Long Drive Home, *Julie Isaac*   199
Facing Death on Kilimanjaro, *Sally M. Veillette*   202
Blizzard Housecleaning, *Stephen J. Hopson*   206
Angels: Don't Leave Home Without Them,
  Doreen Virtue, Ph.D.   209
The Eye of the Storm, *Cathy Adams*   213
Hitchhiking in Europe, *Mary Ellen "Angel Scribe"*   215
A Stranger on a Bus, *Cory Hunter Olson*   217
The Reverend Al Green, *Suzanne Rowe*   219

Contributors   223

ACKNOWLEDGMENTS

I wish to thank those who have supported my dream to birth a collection of mystical travel stories:

Stephanie Gunning, whose vast editorial talents and deep understanding of the mystical made this my best book yet.

Ling Lucas, my literary agent, who believes in me and trusts my dreams.

Rosemary Ahern and Jennifer Kasius at Plume for their willingness to take this journey with me.

Neeti Bahador, Laura Clark, Cliff Edwards, Pearl Fisk, Sheila Fuerst, Howard Fuerst, Teri Garcia, Sharon Harris, Barbara Horner, Katherine Kellmeyer, Jill Lawrence, Carol Rice, Faye Schell, Shelley Schwartz, Alisha Starr, Doreen Virtue—my readers, who took the time to read and score each story. Thank you!

Abbas Nadim of Visions Travel for showing me the best of Egypt and for his assistance in finding stories for this book. If you would like to have a mystical travel experience, call Visions Travel at (800) 888-5509, or visit their Web site: www.visions travel.com. They do fabulous guided tours to sacred sites around the world, including those in Egypt, Peru, Bali, Greece, Israel, Tibet, and India.

Jack Canfield, Mark Victor Hansen, and the Chicken Soup for the Soul team for their continued support.

Ammachi, the Divine Mother, for her contributions to the world and to my life.

Brian Hilliard, my brilliant husband, for his deep love and commitment to my happiness.

INTRODUCTION

I had my first mystical travel experience in 1973. I was a teenager, living in London, attending college. I loved almost everything about London, Tower Bridge, Piccadilly Circus, Hyde Park, the shops of Kensington High Street, the theater, Speakers' Corner, the cultural diversity, the local people, the accents, and even the royal family. My friends and I were among the tens of thousands lining the streets around Buckingham Palace on Princess Anne's wedding day. We waved to her as she passed by in her crystal carriage. I spent many afternoons in the museums and cathedrals, soaking up the beauty and the history. I was adventurous and let my feet just lead me around the city. Since I always carried a city map in my pocket, I knew I would never get lost for long.

One late October afternoon I walked down to the river Thames. I was in a section of the city I had never visited before. I suddenly became aware of the fact that I was totally alone. The streets were devoid of people, cars, taxis, and buses. There was an unusual stillness in the air. I wondered how long the street had been this quiet and why I hadn't noticed it sooner. Then a gust of wind came up off the river. A sheet of old, yellow newspaper blew onto my legs. The headline related to an incident that had happened ten years earlier. I had this feeling that I had somehow walked into a time warp. A few seconds later the wind died down and the street came back to life. I could hear the noise of the city. Traffic began to head down the street. All was normal again.

But where had I gone? What had just happened?

I'll never really know, and I have never been able to forget that day. Something had happened. Something magical, mystical, unexplainable, and exciting. I couldn't wait for it to happen again.

Travel, whether it's a weekend vacation, a trip around the world, or a journey to the inner planes, is an opportunity to experience life outside our usual box. It's a time to taste new foods, meet new people, and discover a world foreign to our daily routine. Why do some people have mystical experiences while traveling? I like to think it's because they have created more time and space for something to happen. When we are living our usual jam-packed daily lives, most of us are too busy or distracted to notice something unusual. Ah, but when we are traveling, part of our goal is to notice everything, even the unexplainable! This is especially true as it relates to "inner" travel, shamanic journeying, dreams, and out-of-body experiences.

Several of my favorite stories in this collection are about traveling to sacred realms or the Dreamtime as the Aborigines call it. This is the land of gods and goddesses, lives past and future, the mysterious and the miraculous.

Whatever way you choose to travel, whether to sacred sites and historic landmarks or into the depths of inner space, remember to make time for a magical souvenir.

—Arielle Ford
La Jolla, California

I

The
Unexplainable

PRISON BREAKOUT

Maggie L. Cooper

Let's call her Janet to protect her real identity. Her trip through time and space began within her prison cell in 1988. Janet couldn't stand confinement for a number of reasons, the main one being that she was unable to go outside for more than an hour a day. To compensate for this deprivation, Janet studied yoga and began meditating.

These practices served as a calming influence that helped her accept the five-year prison sentence she faced. After breaking some prison rule, though, Janet found herself denied any outdoor privileges for two weeks. Heartbroken, she sat down on her cell floor and went into deep meditation. To her surprise, she found herself leaving her body. She passed through the walls of her cellblock and floated over the prison grounds. She passed through the prison wall as easily as she'd left the cellblock. She then drifted upward and floated above the earth.

After what seemed like seconds, Janet gently fell onto the grassy field on her grandparents' farm, a thousand miles from the prison. There she sat, feeling the wetness of the grass and smelling the aroma of the wildflowers around her. She heard the birds singing and watched cows wandering around the field. She touched the grass and the flowers. She picked a golden daisy to smell its fragrance.

Suddenly the cows began moving toward her, as if in a hurry, while in the distance her grandparents called the cows to come to the barn before they locked it. Janet's grandmother walked across the field and stopped at their meeting. "Janet," her grandmother asked, "why are you here?"

Janet's grandmother had been the only person to stand by her when she'd been sent to prison. Her greatest pain was knowing how much she'd made her grandmother suffer. Janet wrapped her fist around the fragile daisy and closed her eyes tight, trying to hold back her tears.

"Where are you going?" Janet's grandmother asked. "Janet, where are you?"

"Janet, where are you?" The frantic voice of her cellmate, Lucy, hit Janet's ears. In the background a metallic voice shouted over loudspeakers: "Prisoner escaped. Lockdown, lockdown, lockdown."

Janet opened her eyes. She was inside her locked cell, sitting on the top bunk. Guards raced along the corridor. Lucy was sitting on a chair, her head in her hands. She seemed to be crying. "Janet, where are you?" she said again.

"I'm right here," Janet replied.

Raising her head, Lucy stared at Janet, and then screamed out, "She's here; she's here!"

The guards ran to the cell and stared at Janet. They walked off, calling out that the prisoner had been found waking up from a nap on her bunk.

When the guards were out of sight, Lucy told Janet, "I know you weren't in the top bunk. I checked it twice. You were missing for almost an hour. We tried to find you before the guards noticed you were gone. I was terrified that you were trying to escape. How did you get back in here?"

"You must not have looked close enough," Janet said. "How could I have got out of this place? I was just in very deep meditation."

With lockdown over and Lucy out of the cell, Janet opened her still-clenched fist. Lying in her hand was the daisy she had picked.

Janet never understood how she had been able to travel to her grandparents' farm that day or how she could bring back that daisy. As hard as she tried, she was never able to make this trip on her own. She pressed the daisy between pages of a book as a constant comfort until she was released. Today she lives in a small house near her grandparents' farm. She visits their field every day in thanksgiving for her momentary and unexplainable release from behind prison walls.

THE MYSTERY OF LOST TIME

★

Gregg Braden

Quickly, I reached under the seat for my belt pack and personal belongings. I could smell the unmistakable odor of hot brake pads as the driver brought our German-built touring coach to a stop. For the last two hours or so, we had negotiated a winding mountain road that became little more than a jeep trail in places. Between the rock slides, blowing sand dunes, and infrequent maintenance, several times the road had narrowed to just a fraction of a single lane. Each time our driver had masterfully eased us through the tight spots, sometimes choosing circuitous detours that always brought us back to the safety of the main roadway. Descending from the village of St. Catherine, located at 4,300 feet above the Egyptian desert, I knew that the checkpoint on the road ahead was near sea level.

The engine, a rest room, and bulging luggage compartments replaced the windows normally located in the rear of a touring bus. Moving to a window, I glanced at the large mirrors on one side of the bus to see behind us. The military truck that had escorted us through the mountains was still there, perhaps two car lengths back. Looking over the head of our driver, I could see that an escort vehicle similar to the one behind us had pulled off the road, near a concrete guardhouse. The camouflaged truck was a troop carrier, the back covered by a dull sand-colored fabric stretched over a series of wire hoops and fastened to the bed of the vehicle. I remember thinking of the similarities between the military trucks in the deserts of Egypt and the covered wagons of the American West that I had seen in museums as a child.

The morning light peeking from behind the mountains suddenly brought the reality of these trucks to life. In the first rays of the desert sun, I could see the faces of soldiers, young Egyptian men peering back at us from their benches beneath the tarp. There were perhaps five men seated on either side of the truck bed; their job was to escort us safely across the Sinai Desert into the massive city of Cairo. Nearly as fast as the local weather changes, the political situation had unexpectedly shifted during our time in the mountains. Now, for our overland route back to the hotel, a checkpoint system had been set up for our safety and to establish our whereabouts at all times. I knew that it would be a matter of only moments before a guard stepped onto our bus, approved our travel papers, and we would be on our way.

Clearing the first of a series of checkpoints, we soon found ourselves winding our way along the brilliant white beaches of the Red Sea toward the Suez Canal. I closed my eyes and imagined the same scene over three thousand years ago, as the people of Egypt traveled a similar route to the mountain we were now returning from. Except for the transportation and roads, how much had really changed? In the warmth of the late morning sun, I soon found myself in conversation with members of our group, anticipating our entrance into the ancient chambers of the Great Pyramid that evening.

Suddenly I looked up as our bus came to a halt along a busy boulevard. From my seat near the front, I glanced through the windows at landmarks to orient myself. To our left was a familiar sight, one that I had seen many times in magazines as well as in person. To confirm our location, I looked to our right. We were stopped in front of a monument that is one of the most powerful symbols to all Egyptians, perhaps of even greater significance than the pyramids themselves: the tomb of the former Egyptian president Anwar Sadat.

As I moved toward the front of the bus, I could see the escorts in front of us. The soldiers had jumped out from under the canopies and were milling around in front of our bus with our driver. Hopping from the last step of our bus onto the street, I noticed something very unusual. The escorts, our driver, and our Egyptian guide, Mohammed, all had puzzled expressions on their faces. Some were tapping their wristwatches. Others were anxiously speaking to one another in short bursts of Egyptian surprise.

"What is happening?" I asked our guide. "Why have we stopped here rather than our hotel, still an hour or so away?"

Mohammed looked at me in awe. "Something is not right," he said, with a rare intensity to his normally playful voice. "We should not be here yet!"

"What are you saying?" I asked. "This is precisely where we should be, on the way to our hotel in Giza."

"No," he said. "You do not understand. We *cannot* be here yet. It has not been long enough since our departure from St. Catherine for us to be in Cairo! It takes at least eight hours for us to make the drive under the Suez Canal, across the desert, and into the mountains. *At least eight hours.* With the checkpoint stops, *we should be even later.* Look at the guards. They do not believe their eyes! It has been only four hours. Our being here is a miracle."

As I watched the men in front of me, an odd feeling swept over my body. Though I had experiences similar to this one when I was alone, it had never happened to me in a group situation. Observing the speed limits, with the extra stops of checkpoints, how could we have improved our driving time by a factor of half?

Though the distance between Mount Sinai and Cairo had not changed, our experience of time while we traveled the distance had. It was recorded on the wristwatches of every military man, armed guard, and passenger on the bus! It was as if our memories of the day, in the presence of one another, had somehow been squeezed into an experience of half the time expected. Where was the rest of our time? Clearly, we were not aware of the phenomenon when it was occurring. The questions are, How did it happen? and Why?

Perhaps herein we find the clue. In our innocence of anticipating the experiences within the pyramids and speaking of the experiences as if we were already there inside the ancient chambers, our awareness had shifted from how long it was taking to *get there* to what it felt like to *be there.*

THE GREAT WHITE SHARK

Jeremiah Sullivan

For over thirty years as a photographer and marine biologist, I specialized in the remote parts of the world, virtually all of them. Many no longer exist as remote, but they were then. I experienced adventures beyond verbal articulation, raw, pure, and perfect interactions with the earth, its elements, and its inhabitants, either above or below the surface of water. Few travels, however, compare to an experience off Australia in 1988. This trip required something very special. I needed a method of travel that would confirm an opportunity to journey back through 10,000 years of human existence, upon the back of a creature 300 million years old.

I hadn't discussed my intentions with any of the other divers before quietly opening the latch and letting the door of our protective cage swing open. The larger of two sharks, perhaps seventeen feet long, had been swimming a slow, regular figure-eight pattern across the bottom. With each pass he came closer. Like a ghostly B-52 bomber, he came so close to the cage that I could feel the displacement of water as he swam past. For some time we observed each other like distrustful siblings, as I noted what seemed to attract his attention or agitate him. Then I slipped out of the cage.

One of my clearest memories as a small child in Hawaii was the discovery of a creature so beautiful but so alien to that familiar shoreline in front of the Royal Hawaiian Hotel that it stopped me in my tracks. It was smooth and clean, a perfectly formed, newborn hammerhead shark. Some kind of visceral genetic recognition seemed to occur. My affinity for the creature was so strong that I wanted to pick him up, take him home, and keep him. That was the first shark I had seen. Even at that early age, I felt a deep appreciation for the magnificent form and physical perfection of these creatures so feared by most other residents of our planet.

Sharks are many things to many people, among them mythical creatures, sacred gods, protectors, and great ancestors. As a marine biologist and naturalist of our time, I'd found the negative, fear-based commentary I've seen from so many experts in the shark research and film community to be wearing very thin and demanding some new thought. It occurred to me that there must be further dimension to the existence of these great fish than we perceive, if we could only reach out to it.

As a result of many years in the water with sharks, I felt that there might be a possibility of friendly encounters with great white sharks. The risk of attempting to find out was incalculable, but trusting some other level of knowing, the noesis, I moved on it.

Our film crew was working for *Mutual of Omaha's Wild Kingdom,* covering some of my research on the predation habits of the great white sharks off south Australia. During the days of filming, sharks usually accompanied our boat, some feeding on the huge chunks of tuna hung from the sides of the hull to attract them, others simply watching and waiting. By day we could see their shadowy figures moving around beneath us, then rising to the surface, lifting their heads out of the water literally to look at us, then slipping silently back beneath the surface. Only great white sharks use visual observation in this way.

At night their dark backs hid their approach until they bumped into the boat with a deep thud that could be made only by a creature of several thousand pounds. Nighttime surface feeding is when the danger feels most unnerving, when attack can occur with no warning from the inky blackness below. All of us were relieved when our night shifts of baiting were over and the bright Australian sun began to warm our backs.

After two weeks of filming the crew got what they wanted, and the assignment was officially completed. Still, we knew there were sharks in the vicinity, including the very big one. The weather was holding well, and the diving was good, so, not quite ready to give it up, we climbed back into our cold wet suits, jumped into the steel dive cages, and gave the signal to lower us sixty feet to the bottom. Visibility was around forty feet on the rocky, weed-covered seafloor as the cages settled just within sight of each other. It wasn't long before the sharks had followed us down and the biggest of them began his cruising pattern.

As he passed, I extended my right hand and let it glide down the massive torso of the great white shark, fully realizing that I was reaching back through all of mankind's recorded experience with sharks. His back felt smooth, like a leather cover pulled taut over an armored vehicle, but with a massive, biological feel to it. His pectoral fins were huge, extending perhaps six feet on either side of his body, forcing me to dodge them as he passed. Drawing on every moment of my years of experience with sharks, I viewed this as a sort of reckoning between us, perhaps a completion of the attraction that began so long ago. Or, even better, a reckoning between the human species and its most feared marine predator.

On his next pass I looped my hand (perhaps unconsciously) over the upper half of his tail, and away we went. Like a streamer in the breeze, I was pulled along in the slipstream of this great white shark. He pulled me effortlessly, powerfully, and faster than a human is capable of swimming. The only acknowledgment of my presence was a subtle but intentional glance at me down his right side.

We continued this mystical tandem until I realized that we had traveled not just the forty feet to the edge of visibility but into the realm of the unknown. I let go and turned to swim back to the rational safety of the cage. Out of the corner of my eye I could see that he, too, was turning . . . and toward me. I tried to accelerate but knew immediately that it was a waste of energy. I stopped. He had broken the figure-eight pattern and, with one flick of his tail, closed the distance between us to only a few feet.

Facing him, and trying to extend my body to appear as large as possible, I prepared for the impact, which had been the last experience of so many before me. I hoped to deflect myself off his massive head and smack him in the gills with my camera strobe, a weighty Subsea MK150, when he reached me. At the same moment that my thought process shifted from fear, or prey, to aggressive combatant, he veered to my right, came to a near stop, and looked at me as if to say, "Oh, Jeremiah, it's you. I didn't recognize you from way over there."

We played that afternoon in a way that must have had Neptune himself grinning in disbelief, swimming together five times for longer and longer distances before I ran out of air. After the initial shock wore off, the other divers piled out of the cages (like tourists off a bus) and began snapping pictures of three different great white sharks . . . in open water. This Friendly Encounter would have been inconceivable to the several other divers who were with me had they not seen it before their very eyes. To my knowledge nothing like this had ever happened before or since that day.

Remarkably, some in the scientific community have expressed little or no interest in the amazing nature of this encounter. Some researchers have suggested that—if it happened—it was a reckless fluke. How sad for them to be interested in science and the exploration of knowledge and yet so frightened of stepping outside what we already know. When opportunities such as this one are presented to those inclined and willing to accept them, old paradigms shift, new thought is born, and this world becomes a better place. All of the necessary elements present themselves to provide that raw, pure, and perfect interaction.

In 1555 Eden wrote in *Descades,* "The tiburon is a very great fysshe and very quick and swifte in the water and a cruell devourer." In 1999 Jeremiah (I am happy to report) wrote, "Not always."

GREEK GHOSTS

★

Stephanie Gunning

I spent my junior year in college on a foreign exchange program in Athens, Greece. Many of our professors were working archaeologists, and we made frequent trips to the ruins of various ancient sites on both the mainland and islands, places such as Delphi and Knossos. During our trip to Olympia, something strange happened to me that I wasn't able to explain until recently.

That morning we had heard a lecture from an expert about the many temples and buildings that had made up this ancient sanctuary in the south of Greece. In antiquity Olympia had been a thriving community whose crown jewel was a magnificent and immense temple to Zeus. Sources reported that the statue in the temple was something like fifty feet high and made of gold. But all that was left on the ground were scattered marble column drums, looking like giant slices of bananas, except each was six feet or more in diameter. Without modern construction equipment, no one knows how this marvel of engineering was accomplished.

My fellow students were having a race in the ancient stadium, re-creating the Olympics, while I wandered off to have a look on my own again at the temple. It was an overcast day and quiet. The air felt very still. In the silence of the moment, I stopped to take in the whole picture of the place. Very faintly the scene changed, like another reality was being overlaid on mine. For a minute or two I was suspended between the two images, and I could see people moving about unaware of me. It was as if I were a ghost in a different time that was still unwinding its course.

A breath of wind, I shook my head, and they were gone. Could it have been my imagination? It felt very real, although translucent.

I never told anyone what I'd experienced. Nearly twenty years later I met a soul healer who works to clear wounds from people's past lives. Among other things, she told me that in one lifetime I had worked as a priestess in a temple in ancient Greece, where I had some conflicts with the authority figures but had led a devoted life. It sounded familiar. I asked her what she actually saw, and she reported that there were images overlaid against the room in which we were sitting.

Olympia must have been a place I once lived in or visited long ago. For a few brief moments, a window opened between this time and that time, and I peeked through.

BOUNCING STONES

Kerry Louise Atlee

There is a very magical place in Queensland, Australia, on the coast somewhere between Cairns and Cooktown in the remote tropical north of the country. I went there with my husband and three sons about six years ago. Even though its location is via a dirt road that is apparently accessible only in a four-wheel-drive vehicle, we happened upon the place in a very ordinary sedan. Our aim had been to drive to Cooktown, really just to say we had been there, but the small sign that signaled this slight detour was far too intriguing to bypass. It read quite simply: THE BOUNCING STONES. We had no idea what to expect.

We got out of the car, kids and all, and off we went. The way I remember it is that we walked onto a beach where instead of sand there were countless stones. They were mostly smooth rocks, easy to hold in one hand, seeming nothing out of the ordinary. But the funniest thing happened as we walked onto this beach of stones; our feet kicked them up and it seemed that the stones themselves were following along with us like excited children who are happy to see someone. I picked up one of them and turned it over in my hands. It didn't look out of the ordinary, just another rock—maybe. But when I dropped it, off it went, ricocheting all over the place. I picked up another one and bounced it like a ball. How could that be? It was only a stone.

My children were enthralled, but there was also a certain air about the place that even they, as little as they were, seemed to respect. I can't put my finger on what it was exactly, but it was like the stones themselves had a life to them, a quality that was very hard to understand at the time. I didn't feel ill at ease about the place, but I did feel something that made me not want to linger for too long. It was as though we were being honored to visit the place. It was, after all, in the middle of nowhere, and the only route to it had been a very unfriendly track across numerous crocodile-infested creeks.

As we walked back to the car, we found another sign that asked people not to remove any of the stones from the area as souvenirs. We were very respectful of that request. It was strange, but I got the distinct impression that taking even one of those stones would be like removing someone's child. I later found out that the site is sacred to the Aboriginals, who have a special relationship with the land. In the Aboriginal Dreamtime, geographic places are considered ancestors and must be respected.

When I told my friends about the site, they all asked why I didn't take just one of those stones, because "nobody would have known." They all added that they would have done so had they been there. But I wonder. I think it's the sort of mysterious place you need to visit to understand that it is more than just a novelty, more than just a quirk of nature. How can it be that ordinary stones can bounce and play and skip along as you walk? I believe there was a form of awareness present.

The bouncing stones are real and, for those who visit, very, very magical. It is a place that will always stick in my mind.

GATEWAY TO ANOTHER DIMENSION

★

Triana Jackie Hill

As my beloved spiritual sister, Lily, and I traveled through Egypt, we had experienced one magical moment after another, and we now, with great anticipation, were approaching the Temple of Karnak. Karnak gave its name to the northern half of the ruins of Thebes, and among its many treasures was the intact tomb of Tutankhamen, which was discovered in 1922.

There are no words to describe the magnificence of the gigantic, perfectly shaped obelisks of the temple, especially the one of Tutmosis I, carved from a single piece of stone that had to weigh many tons. The highest quality of technical execution had been used to create the obelisks and the towering temple pillars, all engraved with hieroglyphics. Lily and I marveled at the exquisitely decorated tombs and reliefs, whose vivid coloring had survived for thousands of years.

After we had spent a great deal of time in the temple, dodging hundreds of tourists, we realized, as we gazed out at the ruins outside the main temple—and saw that only one guard was there—it was time for us to leave each other and be alone for a while. We agreed to meet up again in the late afternoon in front of the temple entrance.

I felt like a speck in the universe as I walked through the massive pillars, leaving the temple. Suddenly my vision got blurry and I was somewhat aware that I was in a trancelike state. My feet felt as if an invisible force were moving them. And then I heard beautiful music in my head, clear, sweet, and bubbling—a celestial concerto of what sounded like nightingales, bubbling mountain springs, and crystalline bells, their tones rising and falling, spinning and gliding in my mind. Then the "music" changed to what sounded like thousands of birds, each singing a different note, that blended together into a cosmic symphony, creating a sense of lightness and beauty that seemed to flood into the farthest recesses of the temple ruins, and bathing the whole area with its crystal, shimmering notes so that, for a moment, I thought I must be in heaven.

In a state of ecstasy, I then heard the deep, mellifluous voice of a man repeating over and over again, like a mantra, "The gateway, the gateway, the gateway," and then a three-syllable word that became a little louder each time it was said, until, with a shiver, I realized that it was my spiritual name, Triana.

My heart filled with joy, my logical mind surrendered to the moment, and I suddenly experienced a burst of energy. In an almost hypnotic state, I fled down the temple steps toward the outside ruins. I stumbled momentarily as the brilliant sunshine blinded me and then set off at a run, ignoring the open mouth of the waiting guard as I followed the length of the wall, heading for the scattered ruins that lay on the far perimeter of the site.

As I left the immediate precinct of the temple, the ground became rougher, and I found myself dodging between fallen lumps of masonry and skipping over fissures in the baked earth. Lizards darted behind rocks at my approach, and a small rodent scuttled nervously into a clump of dry grass as I flew past, drawn as if by a magnet toward the stone solar gateway, which was totally intact. I could now see its massive lintel over the top of the crumbling wall of the ruined building about fifty yards ahead. The gateway was as familiar to me as my name, and I somehow knew that in a previous lifetime I had stood in that gateway.

The sun was beating down on my bare neck and shoulders, and my breath was beginning to come in panting gasps, but I continued to run; the silent call of the gateway was dragging me onward. I rounded the corner of the ruins, and there ahead of me alone in a wasteland of tumbled blocks and shattered columns, stood the sun gate portal. I could now clearly discern what I already knew I would see—the winged sun engraved in the center of the pediment. My legs were aching, but I forced myself across the remaining hundred yards. I didn't even look back to see if anybody was behind me.

As I ran my peripheral vision began to blur so that it seemed as if I were moving down a colorless tunnel whose mouth was framed by the gateway, the rectangle of blue sky, which showed through it, beckoning like the doorway to another world.

The stone arch loomed larger, and at last I was there. I stepped into its center and turned around to face the way I had come, my chest heaving and my knees weak with exertion. For a moment I stood still, too exhausted to do anything, and then, as if in response to some silent command, I raised my arms until they were fully extended and my fingertips were in contact with the masonry on either side of me. Immediately, I sensed a vibration pouring from the stone; my hands and arms began to tingle and the tiredness instantly left me as I felt myself being energized by it. The gateway started emitting a low humming sound. I could feel a massive buildup of energy taking place, as if tiny electrical charges were flying back and forth between the columns.

My whole body was tingling now, and I was beginning to feel light-headed and detached from my surroundings. I glanced dreamily to my right and noticed that I could no longer see the tips of my fingers; it was the same with my left hand. Slowly but surely my fingers were disappearing, as if a pair of invisible gloves were being drawn over them. My hands were no longer visible, and next my wrists, my forearms . . .

I watched my body disappearing, and for some unknown reason I had a total lack of concern as the dematerialization continued. From just above my elbows there was nothing now but empty space. It felt wonderful to be losing my dense body. I thought, What do I need it for? I looked up, and as I squinted against the sunlight, a golden face swam into my vision, smiling its love upon me from the unplumbed depths of its emerald green eyes. "Come with me," it seemed to be saying, as the head inclined backward in a beckoning gesture.

"Yes, I will!" I cried out. "I'm ready to go wherever you go, wherever you want me to!" Again, I felt a great welling up of adoration.

"Triana . . . Triana . . . No . . . you can't go!" Lily's voice rang out across the ruins, and I looked to see my dearest friend stumbling toward me, puce in the face, her features drawn with concern.

Oh, no! I thought. Please leave me alone, Lily. This has nothing to do with you. You can't come with me!

"Triana! You must not go! It's not your time!" Lily was screaming now as she staggered closer. The urgency in her voice interrupted the feeling of bliss I was experiencing. I closed my eyes and tried to ignore the intrusive sound of her voice.

Momentarily the golden face appeared again, smiling, encouraging, but Lily's screams were growing louder and more desperate, and I could no longer block them out.

I hung there, caught between two worlds, and then Lily was in front of me, eyes blazing, as she bellowed, "*Let go!* All that's left of you is your eyes!"

I felt something give way within me. I looked down at my sides. My arms had completely disappeared. In mounting panic I tried to step out of the gateway but could not. The muscles of my invisible legs were frozen.

"I can't," I mouthed despairingly.

With one stride, Lily was in the gateway. She placed her arms around my waist, closed her eyes, and mumbled something under her breath, then, with every ounce of strength she possessed, she heaved backward. For a split second I thought I was being ripped apart. Then, with a crack like a whip, I was released and we both fell heavily to the ground, where, still locked in an embrace, we lay in the dust sobbing and panting.

For some time we remained where we had fallen as I gave way to tears of shock and sobbed like a child, my whole body quivering while Lily stroked my head and murmured reassuringly. At length, my weeping fit passed. We climbed to our feet, dusted ourselves off, and began walking slowly back. I leaned heavily on Lily's arm. I felt drained and dazed, as if I had just been rescued from drowning.

We slowly walked back into the temple and out through the entryway and caught a taxi to our hotel.

Once in our room I collapsed onto my bed, too tired even to take my clothes off. My body felt leaden, yet it was the same body that half an hour ago had felt as light as air and had been dematerializing before my eyes. Christ, I thought, if it had not been for Lily, I would have gone; I really would have disappeared. For a second the true enormity of what had happened sent shivers through me, but then sheer exhaustion took over and soon I was deeply asleep.

. The next morning, when I awoke, my mind spun backward to the mystical moment I had been in the gateway. My heart filled with joy as I realized that I had experienced something very few people, if any on earth, had, and I thanked God for the blessing of my sacred experience . . . one I knew I would never forget! I realized, more than I ever had before, that anything is possible; and since that time I have taught all over the world my Breakthrough . . . Beyond Conception workshops, workshops that have enabled participants to have experiences that also prove to them they can do things they previously thought were impossible!

FINDING PEACE IN TAOS

Pam Brown

Some friends of ours had just moved back to Taos from Cincinnati in September. They invited our family to spend the holidays with them as we were trying to find a way to make it through Christmas, our son Philip's birthday, and New Year's. Philip had passed away that year in October; he would have been seventeen in December. We were not in much of a holiday spirit.

On Christmas Eve we visited a church in Chimayó. Since going there we have done a great deal of reading on the subject, and apparently the church is known for being the site of many miracles. We did not know this at the time. My other two children, Brett and Shannon, my husband, Wayne, and I all said some prayers for Philip. Wayne asked that Philip give us some kind of sign he was okay. He did not tell me this until the next day, but he did tell Shannon that he felt something special was going to happen on Christmas.

We haven't shared this story with a lot of people, since they probably would think we were nuts, but I know what we experienced was real. I remember it today as if it happened last night. It was nothing short of incredible. We have had many other mystical moments, but this, among them all, has brought us the most comfort in our loss. It happened early Christmas morning, and I wrote the following notes about it when I woke up.

December 25, 1995

Wayne woke me up somewhere around 2:00 A.M. saying there was something in the room along the wall behind the bed and chair. There was a column of mist about six feet tall and eighteen inches wide. We questioned if the mist could be from the floor heater Laurie and Ted had mentioned. We later found out the heater was not in that part of the house. The mist was only in that one part of the room. If you stood there or ran your hands through it, it was cooler than the rest of the room.

As time passed, the mist gave way to a different type of substance. It allowed us to see our breath as we exhaled. The air seemed to be alive with some kind of energy. As we ran our hands with fingers open through the air, it was as if they were moving a substance around. We could see the air moving. It was a very dark, purplish black and white substance that appeared only in the spot between the bed and chair. It caused Wayne and I both to feel a good sort of chill and have goose bumps. As we moved our hands through the ectoplasm (for lack of a better word), they looked fluorescent, almost skeletal, with wrinkled skin. Our fingers looked extended by about two to three inches, with an aura appearance. The longer we watched, the thicker the ectoplasm appeared.

We played with the ectoplasm for quite a while, running our fingers, hands, arms, and even our bodies in and through it. We then stood and talked to Philip, and the ectoplasm swirled even more, with a display of thousands of tiny pinpoints of light dancing through the field of energy. The light points were red, blue, yellow, and green, and they left thin trails of white light as they moved.

We both wondered if we were hallucinating, but as we shared what we were seeing, we knew we both were seeing the same things. We were convinced it was Philip answering our prayer for a message from the other side.

This event must have lasted about forty-five minutes to an hour, and it was very emotional for me. From it, I got the sense that Philip is okay.

After about an hour the lights and ectoplasm gradually dissolved. They did not go away all at once. Our hope was that Philip was going to check on Brett and Shannon.

We lay down to try to sleep. After ten minutes, as I looked up in the air, the ectoplasm and lights slowly returned, hovering over the bed. The points of light moved around in the ectoplasm as before. Again we ran our fingers through the ectoplasm and could sense more than air above us. After ten to fifteen more minutes, the ectoplasm gradually dissolved.

Thank you for a beautiful Christmas present, Philip!

THE MOUNTAIN MIRACLE

Deardra Shuler

The little green Volkswagen, occupied by my two brothers and me, made its way along the ice-covered roads and snow-strewn farm region of the Catskill Mountains. We were on our way to school. It was not uncommon for unlicensed farm children in our community to drive as early as ten, helping out the family by driving first tractors, then the family car. Many farms stretched for miles before one could see a neighbor's, and it was a matter of family survival for the entire family to know how to drive in case of an emergency.

My parents were city farmers. My father worked in New York City and returned upstate on the weekends. Our large house sat upon 165 acres of land, and the family was kept busy working the garden, feeding the animals, and picking berries and apples from our orchard to make pies and can jams and jellies.

My mother, who worked part-time as a nurse, would rise early to prepare our breakfast before heading to the hospital twenty miles away, so it was up to my older brother to take us to school.

Although the roads were slippery, because we left late my brother drove faster than usual. I periodically wiped the ice-encrusted windows while my older brother steered the car through the snowdrifts and mounds of snow that towered above us, having been pushed there days before by the county snowplow. The gravel the plow had spread to give traction had long since disappeared.

It is customary to place chains on snow tires as added security when mountain driving, however our tires were without chains. I recognized the need for caution as we approached what we sometimes called Dead Man's Mountain, a dangerously steep hill that had no guardrails to protect drivers from the deep gully below. I asked my brother to slow down as we neared the hill.

"Don't worry about it," he exclaimed. "I know how to drive."

I leaned forward, straining to see through the snow-laden window. "Jimmy, it looks icy," I cautioned in an anxious voice. "I think you should slow down." I glanced over my shoulder at my younger brother, who sat unconcerned in the backseat.

"Calm down. You don't want to be late, do you?" my brother said in an irritated voice.

Those words had barely escaped his lips when the car went into a spin. I grabbed the dashboard in panic. Jimmy slammed on the brakes, causing the car to lurch wildly. Instead of turning the wheel in the direction of the skid, Jimmy instinctively turned it in the opposite direction to try to steady the car. However, the car was no longer under his control, and it headed toward the ravine. My young brother, David, fell forward unhurt into the back of my seat.

The car lunged off the road and plunged into the gully below.

Terror engulfed me. My mind raced; my thoughts were filled with the possibility of our impending death. It occurred to me that either I could face death kicking and screaming or I could relax and go along for the ride. I decided upon the latter.

I said a prayer. I told God that I would accept the fact of my death, if that were to be the case, but asked that my two brothers be spared.

The moment I thought this, I felt great peace. Fear disappeared, and it seemed as if time stood still. It was surreal, like being trapped in a slow-motion movie that suddenly stopped.

Just as suddenly, everything began again. I became aware of time and motion. Although I cannot account for it, our small car was back on the road, completely safe. In fact, we were now miles away from the hill entirely.

"What just happened?" both my brother and I asked in amazement.

We continued to drive to school in silence, each buried in our own thoughts. We never again spoke about what had occurred. What could we have said? What explanation could we have given? There was no explanation for what happened, except to say a guardian angel was watching over us and gave us a miracle that day.

A MYSTERY IN ARABIC

★

Mike G. Doty

The time was late summer 1984. I was working in Saudi Arabia, and my family was living in the States. My wife and I were going to vacation together in Egypt, and I had gone to Cairo three days before her arrival to scout the city and check out places of interest, such as the Cairo Museum, so that her time would be more enjoyable.

The day after she arrived, I took her on a tour of the marvelous Blue Mosque. Since our time living in Europe many years earlier, we have always made it a point to tour old churches, ancient castles, and other culturally symbolic examples of architecture. We had a wonderful time touring the Mosque.

As we were preparing to depart, our guide, who was a very engaging fellow, said that he wanted the "lady" to have a special remembrance of our trip. He offered to show us something not seen by conventional tourists: the crypts of the enshrined leaders of modern Egypt (that is to say, more modern than the crypts in the Valley of the Kings).

The main area of the Mosque is the great rotunda. Hidden from public view and access is a walled area contained at ground level and going all around the exterior of the rotunda. Our guide produced a brass key about one foot in length and asked my wife to open the gates to the crypt area, which we entered with appropriate care and respectful consideration. The guide would show us the crypts of Suleiman the Great, Muhammad Ali Pasha (the last great Ottoman leader in Egypt), and the shah of Iran.

As we stood there in the quiet, our guide mentioned that it was customary for him to say the Arabic Prayer for the Dead before doing anything else. He had got only the first two words out of his mouth when I found myself taking over in a commanding voice I did not recognize as my own. I wasn't in a trance. I wasn't dazed or under the influence of any substance. I simply stood there and recited the prayer, verbatim from the Koran, even though lacking sufficient Arabic to accomplish such a feat.

The prayer was not available in any form of paper handout or on a plaque. I had never previously heard it and certainly would not have memorized the one-minute-or-so prayer even if I could have spoken conversational Arabic. Nevertheless, I finished the prayer.

My wife was understandably impressed, crediting me with having "mastered" Arabic in my time overseas. Our guide was stunned. He also thought I was Arabic fluent. He was very confused to learn that the prayer "just came to me" as we stood there. I could not explain it; nothing had prepared me to speak in that way.

During my remaining years in Saudi Arabia, I had occasion to return to the States on Saudi Arabian Airlines. On every Saudia flight the Prayer for the Dead is recited prior to takeoff. It is clearly a most sacred prayer, but one not of my own religious faith. On many occasions I attempted to follow along and duplicate the mystical incident in the Blue Mosque, but I was unable to do so. Moreover, I remember very clearly that, when saying the prayer in the Mosque, I understood every word I was uttering. Now the words are as foreign to me as ever.

To this day, my wife and I remain mystified by this incident. I have asked several clergy members what they thought about what happened. Their general answer is that it is a mystery not to be questioned. It remains so to us all to this day.

JOURNEY

Micki East, M.A.

Watching Michael as he walked down the hill, I had the strong sense that I knew him, yet this was our first meeting. Our conversation was easy, lasting for hours. Not unlike when good friends meet after many years apart. Who is this man? I wondered. Why is he in my life? Little did I know the journey that lay ahead.

I soon learned that Michael and I shared a fascination with the mystical side of life. Talking on the phone one night, he asked me if I was familiar with the "white light" concept. I shared that I had learned about it in a meditation class. Michael then directed me to look at my left hand. "I'm going to send you some healing white light," he said. "Is your palm glowing?" My palm began to take on a whitish glow. "Now I will make your whole hand glow." I watched in awe as my entire hand brightened.

"How do you do that?" I asked.

"It's easy," he continued. "Just visualize energy coming into your hands, then send it to my hand." I did this, and Michael confirmed that his hand was also glowing.

"Have you ever tried out-of-body travel?" he asked.

"I think I experienced it once during a meditation," I responded.

"I can do it," Michael boasted. "I just imagine sitting on my windowsill and leap off."

Could I do that? I wondered. The next day I received a flyer on an out-of-body workshop. I decided to attend and came back with lots of ideas to explore. Michael was excited about sharing in the exploration, and so the journey began.

That night we agreed to pick a number between one and ten and post it on our dresser mirrors. We would then attempt to leave our bodies, journey to each other's home, and see if we could identify the numbers.

Later I awoke with a jolt. I could feel Michael's presence. I sensed his coming in the door, going to the mirror, looking at the number, and walking back out. Then I imagined being at his house. I could see the paper taped to the mirror, but I could not read the number.

The next day we shared our experiences. Confidently, he shared that he saw the number 2 exactly as I had written it. He then asked me what number I saw. Not wanting to admit I wasn't as successful, I blurted out the number 7.

"Wrong," he answered, laughing. "I know you were here. I could feel your presence. What happened?" he asked.

I confessed that I could not see the number. Michael suggested we try again.

A couple of weeks later I felt the need for some self-healing and began to visualize filling my body with a healing white light. Then I imagined my entire room filled with the light. Suddenly I was aware of Michael's presence. Just as quickly as he arrived, he left.

The next day he called and explained that he had tried to come over. He disclosed that when he had opened the door to my room he was immediately blinded by a bright white light, so he left.

"You could see the white light!" I gasped. "You mean this stuff is real?" He acknowledged it was definitely real to him.

At that moment the white light took on new meaning for me. I began to visualize white light around all the vehicles I traveled in. Before driving anywhere I would map out the itinerary in my imagination, using the light as a guide. If I came to a place on the map where the light got stuck, I would stop and continue visualizing until I could see our car getting through safely.

At first this seemed compulsive to me. But then I experienced a series of events that changed my mind. Using the white light I successfully avoided a head-on collision when a crate fell off a truck in front of my car. Then over the next few months I managed to dodge a deer on the highway and later, by seconds, missing being involved in two serious multiple-car collisions. Recently the white light saved the lives of my son's godparents.

One afternoon while roller-skating with my son, I had the overwhelming sense that something was wrong with my friend Linda and her husband. I remember thinking, I don't know what I would do if anything happened to Linda. Immediately I imagined both her and her husband surrounded by a protective white light. At that moment they were flying in their single-engine plane and the engine suddenly quit.

In the deafening silence that followed, Linda thought about me and began to ask God to white-light the plane. The plane dipped into the clouds, encapsulating it in a white, glowing light. A sense of peace enveloped Linda, and she knew they would be safe. Floating gently down, they came out of the clouds, only to discover they were over an almond grove. Both remained calm as her husband guided the plane between the rows of trees. Although the wings were torn from the plane, they landed. Much to the amazement of all, they walked away from the plane. Linda was unharmed, and her husband had a minor cut on his forehead.

Is the white light real? For me it is. I believe that there is a power and presence that is available to each of us in times of need. If you look with your heart, you can see the soft glow of God's white light inside and around each of us. All we need to do to experience this protective presence is to believe, and it is there.

WILTSHIRE CROP CIRCLE

Victoria Bullis

I've been going back and forth to England from America ever since college because most of my family is English. Because I've been an intuitive since birth, it's always been easy for me, when I'm there, to tune into previous generations and their moments in history. Sometimes I get flashes of the earliest inhabitants doing mundane things such as daily chores in a military encampment or on a farm. By now I am totally comfortable with "knowing" things that happened in any given place, including the ancient power sites, where people have worshiped and sacrificed since nearly the beginning of time.

In the mid-nineties I went back to visit various old friends for a few weeks. I took a train right from Heathrow to Swindon, in Wiltshire, where my old friend Julia picked me up at the station. We dropped off my suitcases at her house and, since it was early morning, she asked me whether I wanted to try to stay up and go out with her while she ran errands, so that I could get acclimated to the time zone, or remain there and take a nap. I was tired but decided to stay up and accompany her.

Wiltshire is the county where Avebury and Stonehenge, the ancient Druid monuments and temples, are. It's also where the famous "crop circles" grow. People have argued for decades about whether these mysterious designs, which seem to appear overnight in the fields, are the work of local farmers being tricksters or that of some extraterrestrial force. I've always believed that they are some of both. I'd been to this area of the United Kingdom many times, and have spent hours traipsing around these amazing sites since my late teens. I am convinced it would be impossible to create at least some of these intricacies by hand during one short night. And I've seen so many over the years that they have become commonplace to me, not a phenomenon.

That morning I was sitting in the passenger's seat, staring out the window, trying to pay attention to Julia's updates on some of our mutual friends, but I was starting to feel pretty jet-lagged. All of a sudden, I sat up straight and cried out, "Whoa!" Julia was so startled that she turned the steering wheel in my direction and we ended up with my half of the vehicle in a shallow ditch. Just as she turned to me and started to open her mouth to express her annoyance, she instead exclaimed, "Oh my God!"

In an instant we both became totally immobile, as though something was holding us down in our seats. Afterward, we agreed that it felt as though an invisible web of some sort had entrapped us. We both saw the same thing occurring in front of us. A crop circle, just to our left, which had at first been in a zigzag design, visibly started to move over to its right a few feet and, as we stared in shock at it, its sharp edges began to soften and become rounded. Amazingly, stunned as we were, neither of us felt afraid; we felt a sense of awe and somehow knew we were safe, protected by a *powerful* energy.

Then, after what seemed like at least a half an hour but was actually only about three minutes, the end of the now-curvy zigzag facing us popped out a little tail, sort of like a comma. As soon as it did that, we were able to move again in our seats.

Julia looked at me and said, "I can't believe we just saw what we did. You've got to promise me that you won't ever tell anyone we know about this or they'll think I'm totally daft." Julia, like most of my friends of many years' standing, isn't "into" metaphysical phenomena and usually tries to pretend I'm not either!

After our initial evaluation of the incident on the ride back to her home, Julia refused to discuss it again, and so I haven't mentioned it since. The next day, anxious to see the crop circle was still there, I talked her into letting me borrow her car. With enormous excitement and anticipation, I drove back to the site and stopped where we'd gone off the road the previous day. Except that now I had a very uncomfortable feeling about trying to tap into what it was that had happened, almost as though some force were warning me off.

I looked at the crop circle for several minutes, took a lot of photographs, and left. None of the photos came out. For the next several days, while I was staying with Julia, I checked all the local papers to see if anyone else had mentioned seeing the same change but didn't find any write-up on it. Local people tend, it seems, to take this stuff for granted.

I haven't been back to Wiltshire since then, although I'm sure I will. For some reason I get a queasy sensation whenever I think about going; I know I was tapping into something otherworldly, which felt safe at the time but certainly hasn't since.

II

Sacred Sites, Synchronicity, and Shamanism

ALIKI'S MIRACLE

Constantin M. Caradimitropoulo

My sister Aliki was born in Alexandria, Egypt, in 1932, and it is because of her experience as an infant that I believe in miracles. Scientists tell me there is no explanation for what happened, so I must believe in the spiritual evidence.

Two or three months after she had taken her first breath, my mother and our French nanny noticed that Aliki was urinating less and less, even though her intake of milk had increased. Ordinarily she should have messed up her diapers five or six times a day, but instead she urinated only a few drops a couple of times a day. Our mother decided to take her to the pediatrician for an examination to determine what was wrong. Dr. Ergeststein, the best pediatrician in Alexandria, was concerned but informed Mother that he could not see or find any blockage and that all of Aliki's vital organs seemed in order. He expressed the belief that the lack of urination was probably temporary but said that she should call him immediately if it persisted and set up a date for exploratory surgery.

My nanny told me years later that my mother's usually jubilant face suddenly turned deathly sick. My mother started crossing herself and calling on all the saints to help her. Knowing my mother, I can visualize it. Although she almost never attended church on Sundays, except for a few holy days, she was a Greek Orthodox and a strong believer in the powers that be.

A week later Aliki still had no urine to speak of and she was turning irritable and cranky. The color and texture of her skin were no longer pink and soft. The whole house was in an uproar, including my aunts Elli and Marika, who started wearing black in the belief that my sister was slowly dying. According to my nanny, a die-hard communist with no religious beliefs, my mother decided that the doctors were incapable of curing Aliki and that their advice to have a priest administer last rites was simply unacceptable.

Mother immediately made plans to take Aliki to the shrine of the Panaghia of Tínos, considered to be the most miraculous saint in Greece. The Panaghia of Tínos is famous throughout the world for miracles that have been accomplished there for Christians, Muslims, and Jews—similar to the Virgin Mary of Lourdes.

The boat trip from Alexandria to the island of Tínos took three days. My mother was a strong woman who believed in herself and her family, but foremost in the powers of miracles. Leaving my father behind, Mother boarded the ship with the hope that, because of her strong belief in the Panaghia, a cure was forthcoming.

I can't tell you exactly when the miracle happened; all I can do is repeat what Mother told me. As the ship was entering the harbor in Tínos, and all aboard could see the beautiful church high up on the hill, my mother watched and prayed to the Panaghia. Suddenly the nanny came running up to her with tears streaming down her cheeks, trying to speak but visibly shaken. Mother's first thoughts were that Aliki had died, and she started shaking the nanny, yelling to her, *"Qu'est ce qu'il arrive, Brigitte? Parle moi, parle moi.* (What has happened? Tell me.)"

"Madame, Madame, venez voir, venez voir. (Come and see)," replied Brigitte. They ran to the cabin to witness the miracle. The bed Aliki was sleeping on was soaked with six weeks of urine, which had turned dark brown from infection. Within a half hour Aliki's pink color returned.

Was it a miracle? Was it the sea air? Was it the grace of the Panaghia? Today I am sixty-five and I still think about Aliki's miracle. Whenever I visit Greece, I always make it a point to pay my respects to the Panaghia and give thanks.

THE STORYTELLER IN KADITA

★

Jessie Heller-Frank

The year I turned fifteen, after my grandmother moved from northern Michigan to the north of Israel, the destination of our family vacation was relocated. I found myself in a foreign country, surrounded by a language I could not speak and a culture I could not understand. After the plane landed and we took a three-hour cab ride, I found myself in a small town in the north of Israel, Tsfat. My grandmother, two aunts, an uncle, and seven cousins now lived there. Tsfat, also called the Mystical City, was the creation site of the Kaballah, the main book of Jewish mysticism. To me it was a small town conducive to nothing I had hoped for in my fifteen-year-old summer.

As most teenagers do, I was going through a lot. Between the changes a girl goes through at that age and life in general, I had many questions; no doubt it was the hardest time in my life. I decided if I ever wanted a healthy relationship and marriage I must first work through and heal my issues with my parents' divorce. I didn't know where to begin. Yet, in a spiritual vortex like Israel, as a question is formulated most likely the answer is soon to follow, and for me it was only a few weeks away.

Toward the end of the summer, my aunt grabbed me late one night, told me to put on my coat, and off we went in a taxi, in the dark, down the mountain. Twenty minutes later we arrived at a village with no electricity or running water. The community was called Kadita, and in the cab I learned we were on our way to a storytelling by a famous Rabbi, Rabbi Shlomo Carlebach.

After we stepped out of the cab, we walked up a grassy hill to a small octagon-shaped hut. Inside people were sitting on the floor shoulder to shoulder. The room, lit with candles, shed a warm rose tone over everyone sitting inside it. I sat down. My back leaned against a canter beam that supported the roof in the center of the room. Across from me was a beautiful, tall, slender young woman. My aunt whispered that it was Shlomo's seventeen-year-old daughter, Dari. She had long black ringlets and a camera around her neck. To my left was Reb Shlomo. He sat with his guitar strapped around his shoulder, wearing a black-and-gold embroidered vest. He played songs and told stories. The night continued into the early hours of the morning, as Reb Shlomo sang song after song and told story after story.

As Reb Shlomo's lips moved, my mind whirled. I stared at Dari intently. By this point, if I had stretched my feet out our shoes would have been touching. I would look at Dari, then back at Reb Shlomo. From child to father and father to child my glances and thoughts took hold of me. Where was my father? I asked myself. Why wasn't he like Shlomo? As I looked at Dari, I meditated on what it must have been like to have a father who embodied Judaism in his every breath—a father who understood the depths of your soul.

I sat there like a teakettle. Everything that had been stagnant inside of me since my parents' divorce got warmed and now was starting to steam up to the surface. The steamlike tears behind my eyes grew as he spoke. The mantra kept repeating in my head all the while: Why isn't my father like that? Why isn't my father like that? Where is my father?

Late into the night, after many stories had been told and many songs had been sung, Reb Shlomo ended. As soon as he stood up, he summoned me to him. I looked over my shoulder to see who he was looking for, but behind me stood only a wall. Hesitant and surprised, I walked over to him. I had met him only once, briefly, and I was sure he couldn't possibly know who I was. "Where is your father?" he asked.

"What?"

"Your father, where is he?"

"He's not here."

"I know, but where is he?"

"He lives in L.A.; my parents are divorced."

"And do you see him?"

"Not so often," I answered. "Sometimes."

Shlomo looked into my eyes, put his arm around my shoulder, and pulled me close to him. "From now on you're my daughter; I'm adopting you. Now you are fifty percent his and fifty percent mine." From his pocket he pulled a card. "Here is my phone number at work and at home. Call me anytime day or night. Now I'm also your abba (father). Dari," he shouted, "come meet your new sister."

He left the house and slowly made his way outside. I could not believe what had just happened. I know I didn't say a word out loud until that point, but he had somehow felt my heart through that crowded room, and heard the tears finally coming to the surface.

How, in the middle of his songs and stories, without any indication—without a momentary lapse in concentration or an unnecessary break in a song—did he recognize my thoughts? There were so many bodies in the room, but somehow he felt mine. As our taxi pulled away that night, I cried. I felt I had just been taken care of on the deepest level, like Reb Shlomo had looked into my soul and saw the part of me that needed healing. And in a moment, he mended it.

When I returned to my uncle's house the next morning, I asked him why he had told Reb Shlomo about my family history. "What are you talking about? I never mentioned it," he responded. I asked my mother the same question, and her answer was that of my uncle. On the plane home I let my thoughts retrace that evening over and over. How could he have known?

A few weeks after arriving home, I was on the phone with my best friend. "You won't believe what happened," she said. "I just read in the paper that, on his way home from Israel, Reb Shlomo Carlebach 'Ztzl' had a heart attack and died." After I had finally been given the father about whom I had dreamed, after only three weeks of adoption, G-d took him from the world. I didn't cry right away, I couldn't; it was all too much of a shock. The tears came much later. In the meantime, something else in my life changed.

The Torah teaches that G-d doesn't take without giving

something in return, and in the following months I watched my relationship with my father transform. As if he had read a letter with every one of my complaints in it, he called up and said, "I think we should spend more time together. I miss you."

The love Shlomo gave me in those few moments in Kadita was enough to guide me forever. He taught me to love my father enough to accept love from him in the way he could give it. When I stopped trying to mold my father into the fanciful character I had decided the perfect father was, Reb Shlomo helped me see that I had the perfect father, one who loved me and was committed to our relationship forever.

Those few minutes with Reb Shlomo changed my life. I learned from Reb Shlomo that if you want a relationship with someone, you have to build a bridge from your heart to theirs, not put a wall in between you. When people ask me about Reb Shlomo, I tell them, "He was a paramedic; he traveled around saving lives."

DREAMER

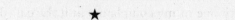

Renu Dudani

A few years ago I went to see an Indian saint named Ammachi, the Divine Mother. My daughter had been quite ill with a chronic disease, and her situation was getting worse. Western medicine had no cure or relief for her, so in vain we tried alternative medicines. Then, through a very reliable source, I heard about Ammachi and decided to give her a try. I myself didn't have any faith in living saints, nor had I ever visited any of them before. But I was desperate, having nowhere else to turn. The results were miraculous, and my daughter started getting better. In fact, she is completely healed today, and all it took was one hug from Ammachi.

Many miraculous things started happening in my life due to Ammachi's blessings, so I decided to bring my parents to meet her at her ashram in India, where they could also experience her blessings. We spent a few wonderful days with Ammachi and then decided to explore the beautiful southern part of India. My parents and I left the ashram by taxicab and went to the nearby town of Alleppey to spend the night on a boat. The captain told us he was Ammachi's neighbor, and everyone we met in the town said they knew Ammachi. Early the next morning we hired another taxicab to take us into the mountains.

Halfway to our destination the taxi began to overheat from the climb. The driver pulled over to get some water from a waterfall to cool down the engine. I decided to go in search of a bathroom. In just a few minutes I found a bathroom in a small building surrounded by trees. This bathroom was totally spotless (very unusual for India), one of the cleanest bathrooms I have ever seen, especially since we were literally in the middle of a jungle.

Since we had left so early in the morning, we hadn't had time to eat breakfast. I was now very hungry and began to crave idli-sambhar, which is a South Indian dish that I have always enjoyed but hadn't eaten during our stay. I asked a man who seemed to be in charge of the place if he knew whether there were any restaurants nearby. The man suggested a place—one that would take us just slightly out of our way. I told our driver about it, and he said that he didn't think there was any place to eat in the vicinity. The driver said that he drove this route nearly every day and he had never seen such a place. But, because we were all so hungry, he decided to follow the directions. Just as the man had described, we soon came upon a guesthouse with a sign out front that said, DREAMER.

In many ways this guesthouse was like something from a dream. There were no other guests, just the eight servicemen who worked there. The house was very warm and hospitable and reminded us of a home we had lived in thirty years ago in the village of Balaghat, India. This had been a large British home, almost a mansion, with thirteen rooms and many servants, and this guesthouse looked almost identical to it. Much of the furniture and many of the accessories and plants were very similar to the things in our old home. My mother was astounded—even the servants had the same "feel" as those from our previous home. Being at Dreamer brought back very pleasant memories for all of us.

The host offered to serve us lunch. He said that although they normally had a large menu, today the only dish they were offering was all-you-can-eat idli-sambhar, for twenty-two rupees. I remember thinking, Well, I was just wishing for some idli-sambhar, and what a great price. Twenty-two rupees is the equivalent of fifty cents—an extremely good price for a guesthouse meal—and all-you-can-eat is not something one finds in India. The three of us enjoyed a wonderful meal.

Halfway through the meal the waiter said to me, "Would you like your hot water now?" That's when I began to get suspicious. Drinking hot water with a meal is my personal custom, but no one in India drinks plain hot water—especially in a hot tropical state like Kerala, where everyone drinks cold coconut juice or

Coca-Cola. Even my father got suspicious and said to me, "Why did he ask you about hot water now and not me? How did he know? How come he didn't ask me about any coffee or tea?"

Then I began to laugh. Something inside me realized that Ammachi was giving us a clue that she had created this Dreamer for us, to let us know that she was satisfying our needs and to build our faith that she would always provide exactly what we need.

The waiter brought me my hot water and also gave me a thermos of hot water to take for the ride. I asked the staff how long the guesthouse had been open, but they vaguely said, "Just a short while."

It was now time to leave. My mother was so comfortable that she wanted to cancel all of our plans and spend the rest of our vacation at Dreamer. We finally convinced her that we needed to continue on our way. The rest of our trip was filled with magic and coincidences, and we felt Ammachi's presence with us throughout. Still, even to this day, I wonder, if I went back to that mountain road, would Dreamer still be there?

A MERSEYSIDE MIRACLE

Kathleen McGowan

I was still a teenager when I learned the secret formula behind miracles: that unshakable belief combined with clear intent leads to a miraculous outcome.

I was seventeen years old when one of my beloved heroes, John Lennon, was gunned down in New York City. My teenage heart was broken by this act of savage cruelty. John Lennon's death became a rite of passage for me, an event that marked my ascent into adulthood. As the assassination of John F. Kennedy impacted my parents' generation, so the murder of a beloved Beatle and peace activist affected me and mine.

My best friend from childhood, Della, made a pact with me shortly after Lennon's death; we were determined to travel to Liverpool as soon as possible, to celebrate John's life. The horrifying death of our hero had an even more disturbing significance for Della—it had occurred on the evening of her eighteenth birthday, while we were out celebrating. Seven months later, we were waiting at a London train station to depart for the famous birthplace of the Beatles.

Nineteen eighty-one was a tumultuous year in England. Race riots had erupted in Brixton and Liverpool, while the tensions of Northern Ireland were boiling over in the Irish-dominated Merseyside. On the morning we were scheduled to leave there were dire advisories about travel to Liverpool. The rioting had reached a fever pitch the day before, with serious casualties.

As we waited to board the train, a sweet little man approached and asked us about our destination.

"We're going to Liverpool," I exclaimed proudly.

His face fell. Gently but firmly he explained that the current social climate in Liverpool was not terribly welcoming for two

young American girls. Didn't we understand that people were
getting killed up there? Why didn't we stay in London and do
some wonderful sightseeing or shopping? he suggested.

We laughed at him, Della and I. Eighteen years old and fearless, we possessed the blissful teenage certainty of absolute im-
mortality. We told him that we weren't afraid and would not be
dissuaded; we had come to England to visit Liverpool specifi-
cally. Our intent was completely clear, to see where the Beatles
were born and to celebrate the life of our fallen idol. This was a
pilgrimage of sorts, and our belief was unshakable. We would
accomplish our intent in absolute safety.

Thank you so much for your concern, Mr. Nice Old English
Man, but if it's all the same to you, our train is about to depart.

We boarded the train and quickly discovered that the sweet
old man who had attempted to talk us out of our folly was in
fact the train's conductor. We fidgeted for the three-hour journey
on the train, restless with the spirit of adventure. We had no
plans when we arrived in Liverpool—nowhere to stay, no means
of transportation. Just the absolute belief that we would fulfill
our intent. As the train moved closer to our destination, a voice
came over the loudspeaker. It was the sweet old conductor: "For
my two little American friends who are willing to risk their lives
to see where the Beatles were born, that is the famous Mersey
River on your left. Welcome to Liverpool, girls!"

Della and I giggled at his sweet message and reveled in the
nearness to our destination. It was a matter of only minutes before we were approached by two very American-looking men.

"Are you the two crazy American girls here to visit Beatles
country?" they wanted to know.

"And proud of it!" we exclaimed.

The two men exchanged a look before introducing themselves. They were a reporter and a producer from NBC's *Today*
show on their way to an assignment—to do a story on American
tourism to Liverpool. One angle they were anxious to explore
was the impact of John Lennon's death in terms of travel to
Beatles-related destinations.

They asked us if we would be interested in helping them out.
Sure, we agreed casually, as long as it doesn't interfere with our

intent. They exchanged another look and smiled. Then they made their offer: they would provide us with a chauffeured car, local guides who had grown up with the Fab Four (including the Beatles' first manager, Alan Williams), and they would take us absolutely anywhere we wanted to go. The only thing they wanted in return was the right to place hidden microphones on us and to film our natural reactions to the sights. Oh yeah, they also offered to pay all of our expenses in Liverpool, everything from food and drink to admission to the new Beatles Museum.

The result was an absolute dream come true for two teenage girls. We were hand-carried through the city of Liverpool, from Penny Lane to the house where John was raised by his Aunt Mimi. We heard Beatles anecdotes from their childhood friends and visited places we would never have had access to otherwise. All the while, the reporter Eric Burns and his crew treated us like royalty.

If we had arrived in Liverpool on our own, most of the sights we had come to view would have eluded us. We had not anticipated the size of the city and were too young to rent a car. Public transportation, including the taxi system, was partially suspended because of the rioting of previous days. But the clarity of our intent and the power of our belief manifested a magnificent—even a miraculous—outcome.

The *Today* show aired a few weeks later. There we were, two young pilgrims climbing around Aunt Mimi's flower garden, celebrating the life of the man who grew up there and influenced millions with his music and message.

Imagine.

THE GODS LOOK DOWN

Rik Cooke

Spring 1989

My sister, Maria Luisa, was on the phone to inform me that her Argentine brother, Miguel de Herrera, was going to be traveling around various countries of Central America. "He and his partner, Alejandro, will eventually get to Mexico. Won't you be there on your National Geographic assignment? It would be so nice if my two brothers could finally meet."

Our mother and my stepfather, Luis, had both been married previously and had children by their original spouses. Unfortunately, when my two brothers and I moved to Argentina, Luis's former wife, an ardent Catholic, forbade her children to meet us. Luis saw no reason to punish his children in this way, but she was adamant. In time, two of her daughters braved their mother's wrath and visited our family regularly. We all became loving friends; however, Miguel, the youngest and easiest to control, was too young to protest.

In Buenos Aires we attended St. Andrew's, a highly respected Scottish school, and thoroughly enjoyed life in Argentina. Especially the huge daily steaks. Our sister Maria Luisa was born, but our joy was short-lived. When she was just nine months old, her father died tragically. It was a terrible blow to all of us, and a year after Luis's death we left the Argentine and returned to California to live.

So time and distance had kept Miguel and me from knowing each other. I agreed it would be great if we could meet, but I tried to explain how the logistics might be difficult to organize. "I'm traveling mainly throughout northern Mexico, visiting ancient sites. I have a car and driver, and stay in each place depending on what I find there. If it's not interesting, I move on to the next place. The only fairly definite date I have is when I get to Mexico City to meet an anthropologist, a geologist, and an archaeologist, all sent by Geographic to assist me while I photograph ancient relics in the famous Anthropological Museum of Mexico City.

"This will make up an important chapter for the book *Ancient Cities of America,* for which I am the sole photographer. Usually there are four photographers for each National Geographic book, so this is a big responsibility. I'd love to meet Miguel. I know how much you adore him, but it seems impossible to plan."

Several weeks later I arrived in Xochxicalo, a pretty esoteric Aztec ruin that few tourists visit. Outside of Veracruz, it has no headquarters to contact and needs to be carefully scheduled. My driver, Manuel, assured me he could find the ruins, and so far he'd been terrific. He drives all the National Geographic people who come through there. I particularly wanted to see the Ball Court, where the Aztec games were held, and the Pyramid of the Serpent, known for its relief carvings, so we made our plans.

Once there we climbed to the top of the pyramid, which looked out over the old city ruins below. The place was totally deserted, not a soul in sight. A native guide, looking like a Mayan himself, with the pronounced aquiline nose, spotted us. He quickly gave my driver the pitch, saying he was the only guide there and he could speak English. He added that two Argentine doctors had already hired him but that I could join them while he escorted them through the ruins.

Shortly two figures were seen approaching the pyramid. I watched as the two M.D.s came up the steep slope. One had a mustache and bright red hair. The other was slim and blue-eyed, and bore a striking resemblance to Maria Luisa. As they came up to where we were standing, I went to him and said, "You must be my brother Miguel."

I can only imagine the shock he felt when a six-foot, four-inch tall giant weighing over two hundred pounds, wearing an Indiana Jones hat and loaded down with cameras, approached him with such a remark.

With a look of astonishment, he responded, "You must be Rik."

I stepped forward and gave him a big *abrazo* (embrace), which nearly bowled him over.

After recovering from his surprise, he couldn't have been more friendly. He introduced me to his friend, who diplomatically became scarce, and we spent much of the next two days getting to know each other. I found him to be totally delightful.

So finally, after thirty years, we two half brothers of my sister met. It was to be the first of many happy meetings. The whole thing was so incredible. There is no way it could have been planned. I'm convinced the ancient gods had a hand in this.

SICILIAN
SYNCHRONICITIES

★

Rosanne M. Siino

We were eating dinner with Sally's relatives in their modest villa in southern Sicily when Sally, my energy-worker pal, looked me in the eye and said, "Tomorrow in your father's village, I see us having dinner with a bunch of your Siino cousins." I nodded and smiled politely, but inside I was thinking, Fat chance, Sal! I didn't have any names of relatives to look up, any addresses. Heck, I didn't even know if there were any Siinos in Isola delle Femmine anymore.

You'd think I'd know better than to doubt Sally.

Sally and I had met climbing Mount Kilimanjaro in Africa earlier in the year. That was a trip filled with miracles, not the least of which was getting me—the nonathlete of the group—to the top! Sharing that adventure had forged a strong bond between us, one that would probably last a lifetime. So when Sally invited me to Sicily in the summer—the place where my father had been born—I knew I had to go. Sally knew how to trust the Universe to deliver the things that needed to happen—and that was a lesson I was ready to learn.

My father had died twenty-seven years earlier, when I was just a child, and my memories of him were as faded as old photographs left too long in the sunlight. The only thing that remained vivid for me was a sense of loss—a loss that heavily colored my perceptions and my relationships this many years later.

While I had no specific idea of what I wanted to occur, I held a hope that somehow on this trip with Sally I'd find some healing and connection with the father I had only briefly known.

Planning? Well, that's never been my strong suit. As I men-

tioned, I had done nothing to find out whether I still had relatives in the area, or where I should go to learn about my dad,
who had immigrated to America with his parents when he was
just a boy. Yet when we drove the four hours across Sicily to my
father's town in a rickety old Lancia borrowed from Sally's
cousin, I tried to be open to any possibility. And we were in the
heart of Isola delle Femmine for only thirty minutes before the
Universe filled in for the planning I didn't do.

It started in the most unlikely of ways. Looking odd and out
of place in the old town's only piazza was an Internet café—and
I, an Internet addict, jumped eagerly at the chance to send e-mail
home from my father's birthplace. So in I went, leaving Sally
alone to meet and talk to various salami makers, the dress shop
owner, and the produce guy, who also had their businesses
around the piazza. Finally done with e-mail a little later, I found
Sally chatting with a young mother, and I jokingly asked whether
she knew any Siinos in town.

Sure enough, she did! She said a widow with that name lived
up just a few blocks (at least, with our limited Italian, that's
what we thought she said!), so Sally and I thanked her and went
to check it out. While I had no idea what we'd do when we got
there, I was with Sally, and she wasn't about to stop and think
about such minor details.

We found a street that seemed like a likely candidate and
began looking at doorbells. Almost immediately we found one
with SIINO alongside it, and before I could muster the courage to
ring the bell, voices called down to us from a balcony above,
asking who we were looking for. We told them in our bad Italian that we were looking for a Siino family and tried to explain
who I was. Evidently, our Italian really was pretty bad, because
one of the old men said in broken English, "Hey, you from
America? Come up here and we'll figure out who you are. . . "

Well, coincidences continuing, it turned out that the widow
had a son who spoke perfect English and was, at that minute,
coming home for the evening from his job as a fisherman. He
and the older man had lived for years in Monterey, California—
less than an hour from where I lived! We chatted easily about ge-
nealogy, figuring out our connections, and before I knew it we

were—as Sally predicted—sharing a wonderful and warm Italian dinner with my cousins!

But it didn't end there. They insisted on driving us after dinner to meet another Siino family more closely related to me; with them we shared many laughs as we figured out our lineage, as well as tons of sweets and plenty of Fanta soda (the Italian drink of choice when you aren't drinking caffe, vino, or grappa). While my Italian was poor, the faces of my cousins were welcoming and excited, making verbal communications almost unnecessary. We all took pictures and exchanged addresses (e-mail addresses, of course!) before Sally and I headed out.

As we drove back to Sally's town, I sat mystified. With no information or planning, that night I had made connections that were richer than anything I could have imagined. While I still carry the loss of my father, that evening I felt my first real sense of belonging and peace. It was as though, in his hometown, I could see my father's face shining through the eyes of my cousins. And it was then that I knew I'd finally experienced what it means to be at home.

BUTTERFLY MAGIC AND
THE MOODY BLUES

Alan Moore

On August 5, 1993, I was invited to a butterfly garden at the Green Lane Nature Center not far from Allentown, Pennsylvania. When we arrived, there were hundreds of butterflies fluttering about a profusion of fragrant flowers, shrubs, and herbs. I felt connected to nature through the wonder of all that was around me. Something stirred my deepest emotions. Like a child again, I likened the scene to something right out of *Alice in Wonderland*. I left that garden determined to create similar gardens for children everywhere. Beautiful butterfly gardens for children of all ages.

On my way home I listened to my new tape, a mix of songs by John Lennon, Joan Baez, the Moody Blues, and other sixties artists. Suddenly I realized there were butterflies in the music that I never heard before. I had made a butterfly tape before I'd even had the experience! The music and the image of the butterflies gave me an epiphany—a thousand lights all lit at once. I had a brainstorm to use the butterfly as a symbol for the environment. It would be better than the Save the Whales campaign, I told myself. "You can't take a whale to a school yard, but you can plant a butterfly garden there." Everybody could attract butterflies to their homes, schools, and parks, and have a personal experience with nature like the one I had.

It seemed an impossible dream, but I didn't care. Somehow I knew it could be done. "It's going to be hard," I told myself, "but who else will do it?" Have you ever had that feeling? My mind jumped to life, and soon it was pregnant with the possibilities, potentialities, and probabilities of this endeavor. I was ready to commit myself.

I had a sudden sense of sacredness and great urgency. I broke out in goose bumps as I wondered why. An intuitive voice deep inside came to me. "No room for ego if you're dealing with something sacred. Just stand back and let the whole thing flow and unfold on its own." My rational mind told me I was just daydreaming, yet I disagreed. If my vision were true, it would manifest itself. It would happen if I believed and had faith that it was real.

When I arrived home, I told my wife that I was leaving my job. I was shedding my responsibilities as if I were a caterpillar shedding its skin, getting rid of the old in preparation for the new. By the end of the day, I had the goals for a new organization put down on paper, the Butterfly Gardeners Association, or Bee Gees for short.

Over three years, I achieved most of the goals I set out to accomplish. Everything began to fall into place—intuitive, synchronistic, and mystical stuff started happening every day. This continued until February 1996, when I put my project into a cocoon. I had spent everything I had saved and gone into debt. However, when I didn't work on butterflies and went back to work to earn money, all the magic stopped. Then, in October 1996, I brought butterflies back into my life and the magic started again.

My daughter was dating a boy named George. One Sunday morning, I got a call that his father had died. The funeral would be on Wednesday. That same afternoon, as I was strolling in my garden, I came across a monarch butterfly. It was late in the season for a monarch. They should all have migrated by then.

In the past, I had raised monarchs for people to release at funerals. The butterfly is a symbol of the soul passing on. I wanted to do a butterfly release for the upcoming funeral. That could have been the last monarch I would see, but I didn't want to catch it and keep it imprisoned in a box for three whole days. So I let it go.

On Tuesday, I went out looking for any kind of butterfly. The whole day was gone and no butterfly. The sun was getting low in the sky. My wife came home, and both of us looked around for the last time. We realized that nothing was going to happen; you don't find butterflies at night. I followed my wife toward the house. As she went in, I stopped and closed my eyes and thought, Please God, I need a butterfly by tomorrow. I needed some butterfly magic.

When I went inside, my wife was on the phone with a woman who told her that she had just found a monarch at her doorstep. She was concerned because it was so late in the season, so had called me to come and take care of it for her. My wife, who had been skeptical about butterfly magic, was amazed.

I threw on a monarch T-shirt and went to pick it up. The first thing the woman said when I arrived was "I have the same T-shirt!" The magic of synchronicity was back and, of course, it was all about butterflies. The butterfly had landed in her yard, the yard of a butterfly lover. She had thought to call me on the very evening when I was especially looking for a butterfly. I took the butterfly home, made a sugar-water solution, and hand-fed it. It became active after eating and flew around the house. I put it to sleep for the night in a dark cage of its liking.

The next day at the funeral, I released the monarch while reciting a prayer about spirit flying free from Marianne Williamson's book *Illuminata*. The butterfly took off straight up in the air and disappeared in a flash. People came up to me later and said it was the most beautiful service ever. They felt that the soul had left on the wings of that butterfly.

George said he needed to be alone for an hour at the grave site. As our family was walking to the car, I kept looking back and wishing that the butterfly would appear again. On the way home I told my wife that I thought something magical was going to happen. The night after I lost my aunt, I had felt her presence walking down the hall. Now I had the same feeling again.

Here's what happened. George called us later. On his way back from the cemetery he stopped at a light, and a monarch landed next to his car. It was an area under construction, not a place where you normally see a butterfly. When the light turned green, the butterfly flew right along with his car and kept pace with him. As the butterfly followed him, he broke into bittersweet tears.

When he got home, George opened his door and for a moment saw his father sitting there. He took great comfort from it. I believe the monarch that followed him home was the soul of George's father, coming to let George know that his father was still with him and always would be.

JOURNEY BY WATER

Stephanie Gunning

A couple of years ago I took a workshop on Celtic shaman-ism, the religion of the ancient people of Scotland, Ireland, Wales, and the Isle of Man. My family has some Irish and Scottish roots, but I don't know much about them. In this class we were going to learn how to journey to the spirit world, find the assistance of animal spirit guides, and receive answers to questions from the spirits about our lives and destinies. Because I am a book editor, I had been invited to attend the workshop to learn more about the subject matter of a manuscript I was working on. I was also eager to see if I could actually achieve a direct communion with mystical beings—I wanted advice.

On the first day the shaman priest who was our leader gave a talk about the levels of the world. She explained that in her cosmology the earth where we live is the middle level, but you can pass through invisible barriers that go to upper realms and lower realms. Different kinds of spirits and deities live in each place. Most of them want to help human beings, because that's what they do. They have awesome powers that living people do not because they are made of energy not matter. She reminded us to be respectful and honor the beings we met.

For our first journey, we would go to the underworld and ask our spirit guides to reveal themselves. Everyone has at least one animal guide, some more. Once I met my guides, they could help me get around. My body wouldn't actually go anywhere, but I would travel through my imagination to a reality that was parallel. Just as our world has gravity and an atmosphere, the other world has distinct conditions and rules of existence. These might not seem logical.

I was eager to journey and nervous at the same time. What

animal would my spirit guide look like? A bird? A tiger? An elephant? I felt like an adopted child about to meet her birth mother.

After we did a brief ceremony—lighting candles and chanting a call on the spirits to assist us—we were ready. The group lay on the floor and covered our eyes. There was a drummer, who beat a steady, galloping rhythm that produced an urgent expectation. Our instructions were to see a tree in our mind's eye, either to get very small or to see the tree get very big, and then to enter its trunk and travel down through the root, where we would come out into the lower world. During this journey we should keep asking our guides to reveal themselves and help us through. Once we knew the route, the shaman told us, we would always be able to go back and forth the same way. The whole journey was to take about fifteen minutes.

The drummer was drumming. I saw a large pine tree that was on some property my family had once owned. I went toward it and imagined myself inside the trunk, getting smaller and smaller, going down into the root, and then . . . I got stuck. It was pitch black, I couldn't see, and I wasn't making any progress. Over and over I said, "Spirit guide, are you here? Would you show yourself? Please, help me." I felt desperate to move. What if I couldn't get there? My heart was beating in frantic time to the drum. I renewed my efforts, but it didn't seem that an act of will was working. Then I felt my nose begin to twitch and my hands turn into paws with long, pointed nails. It was as if I had transformed into a rabbit or a rodent trying to dig my way through. I also felt the presence of another being, but it wouldn't answer me. If my guide was there, I couldn't see it in the darkness. Finally, I thought I saw a faint light at the end of the root, and it was as if I had emerged in a field on a moonless night. But I convinced myself it must be a fantasy. Then I heard the drum calling me back. I had failed either to meet my guide or to get to the other world.

What a bummer! Many people had done this before. Of the newbies, everyone else had made it, and they were excited and eager to tell what had happened. This one's guide was a falcon. That one's guide was a wolf. The shaman said that I had shape-shifted, and that meant I must have made more progress than I thought. I was disappointed and glad to break for lunch. The shaman reassured me that we would journey again that afternoon—it is quite common not to find one's way the first time.

That afternoon we lay down on the floor again and closed our eyes. The drumming started. This time we had an assignment to go to the underworld, meet our guides, and visit one of our ancestors to ask an important question. I was so determined to make the journey that I decided to get a really good look at the tree and then run toward it and throw myself down the root. I couldn't come up with a better plan. As I was backing up to get a better view, I stumbled into something behind me. I turned around and realized I had bumped into an old well. I had completely forgotten we had one in the middle of our yard.

I suddenly got an inspiration. The well went downward— maybe I could swim to the underworld. I leaned over, took a breath, dove in headfirst, then swam rapidly down through the cold, clear water, which soon opened into a larger space. I continued swimming up toward the light of day and easily emerged in the middle of a vast lake. I had made it! But where?

The next thing I knew, I was joined by a frolicking dolphin— or was it a porpoise? I remembered that there was some difference between the two creatures. It was my guide! I greeted him. "Hello. Are you a dolphin or a porpoise?" He answered, "I'm a porpoise with a purpose." (It figured I had a guide with a sense of humor.) I took hold of his dorsal fin, and he happily pulled me behind him, swooping and spinning at play through the sparkling water. He seemed to know exactly where I needed to go. I was just along for the ride. It was exhilarating and mind-blowing to be at one with this powerful creature, really feeling the texture of his skin and the ripples of the water's displaced surface coursing over me. We traveled impossibly fast and within a minute or so had reached an island in the middle of the lake.

I let go of my guide and waded up onto the shore. Walking through a dappled forest, I came upon a clearing, where I saw a luminous white light. I was in the presence of a spectacular woman in flowing robes made of a gauzy, floating fabric, with hair so light it was white. It was exactly like a fairy tale. She was

smiling with joy that I was there. Her whole being evoked benev-
olence. Naïvely I asked, "Are you my ancestor?" She didn't say
anything, just laughed at the silliness of my question. I realized
as soon as I said it that, of course, I was in the presence of a
deity. But I had no name for her, since I knew nothing about
Celtic divinities. She was so beautiful that seeing her was like
watching sunlight twinkle inside a diamond.

I didn't know why the porpoise had brought me here, so I
asked. Her answer resonated within me without words. She
loved me and was going to help me. "I need to meet my ancestor," I told her.

In a blink I found myself inside a room made of stone looking out a window over a town by an ocean—or maybe it was at
the edge of the giant lake I hadn't thought that the spirit world
would be inhabited, but this town had a working population.
People lived there. I could see fishermen down by the shore hauling nets and pedestrians moving about. And I realized I was not
alone in this room. There was a middle-aged man there, with
short hair and glasses. His face seemed close to mine, although I
think he was standing across the room. I was mesmerized. He
didn't look like any relative I had ever met, but for some reason
I believed he was my great-grandfather on my father's side. The
room had very few furnishings. I noticed a small wooden table
that was set for lunch. It was as if I'd interrupted his meal.

My ancestor looked me in the eye, but he never said a word.
Time was running out, I would soon hear the drum call me back.
I had to ask him my question now. "What must I do to be a re-
sponsible member of our lineage? Is there anything I must do for
our clan?" And the answer came wordlessly back, "You've already done it." He took me by the hand, and when I looked
down at my right arm it was glowing red from my fingertips to
my elbow. Pulsing with red energy. Wow!

I heard the drum calling me, my clue to leave. So I thanked
him, then ran to the water's edge and dove in; the porpoise met
me and swam me back to the well, where I also thanked him for
his help. I traveled up through the well and out, opened my eyes,
and I was back at the workshop.

What was really weird was that when I touched my arm, it

was actually hot. No one, not even the shaman priest, knew exactly what that meant, but everyone agreed that my journey had been significant. Not only had I met my guide, the lovable porpoise with a purpose, but I had met a benevolent goddess and my ancestor. I learned that I have no outstanding obligations to my family and lineage, and that my right arm has some significance for me—perhaps because I am a writer.

Since then, I have journeyed many times to the lower world and the upper world. To get to the upper world I must climb a vine. Most Celtic shamans travel through the roots and branches of plants to reach their destinations, but I have met one other, like me, who enters by another route: he goes to the lower world through a cave. I am grateful to God for assistance in finding the well between the worlds. My sacred animal guides and bird guides help me travel over land and through the air, but my easiest passage is always the journey by water.

THE MYSTERIOUS MAYAN SHAMAN

★

Jill V. Mangino

I did not know much about Mexico or the Maya. However, when I first received an e-mail about the Prophets Conference being held in Mexico on the fall equinox of 1998, I knew I had to go. Something inside of me was pulling and tugging to make this a reality.

The following day, I was still not sure if I should register for the conference, so I approached my extensive "metaphysical" bookshelf, closed my eyes, and pulled out two books. This is a fun thing I like to do when I'm looking for a sign from the Universe. The first one I opened to a page that had a map of Mexico. Okay, well, that's a pretty good sign. The next book I turned to was a book by Graham Hancock; sure enough (eyes still closed), I opened up to the chapter about Palenque, a Mayan ruin. Goose bumps ran up and down my body. I was looking for signs but not that profound! Wow! Now there was no turning back—I was going to Mexico.

I arrived in Mérida, Mexico, with a deep inner knowingness that something magical was going to happen. I easily made friends as we journeyed to several sacred Mayan ruins for ceremonies led by Elder Hunbatz Men, a representative for the Maya Itzae (from the Yucatán Peninsula). I also was happy to reconnect with several friends from Hawaii who likewise felt divinely guided to attend the conference.

On the third day of the conference we traveled to the Mayan site of Dzibilchaltún and, after a group ceremony around the sacred cenote (a sacrificial water well), we all climbed the pyramid and chanted at the top. It was here that I noticed a mysterious shaman who was not part of our group. He was dressed in white, wore a large turquoise choker, and was holding a quartz crystal wand. This extremely handsome and intriguing man fascinated me. He felt familiar, as if I knew him from somewhere, yet I knew we had never met. As I vacillated over whether or not to approach him, I heard a voice inside my head that said, "Do not approach him now." As odd as that seems, I have learned to listen to that "little voice." I held an inner dialogue with myself and questioned, "What if I never see him again?" However, I let go and trusted that, if it was meant to be, it was meant to be.

The next day we loaded up our tour buses, all 150 of us, and went to Chichén Itzá, one of the more well known sacred Mayan sites. Thousands gather here biannually to witness the Descent of Kukulkan. Tourists can witness this phenomenon, in which a perfect geometrical shadow, in the shape of a serpent, mysteriously descends upon the face of the pyramid during the spring and fall equinoxes.

While in Chichén Itzá, I left the group for a while and found myself in a meditation temple. In deep contemplation, I noticed that my heart felt closed. I knew that until it opened up I would not feel a deep connection in this place. Others were having profound experiences and I felt nothing. As I was thinking these thoughts, a warm energy began to penetrate my heart; within an instant I began to weep, actually sob, for almost fifteen minutes. It was an amazing healing experience; I felt my heart expand; it was as if something heavy had been weighing on me and was lifted, and a deep remembrance overwhelmed me.

As I left the deep, dark, cavernous, ancient temple I began to see with new eyes. I felt connected to this land, to this country, to the people. I made a point to embrace as many members of our group as I could. I was filled with joy. However, I was sadly disappointed that the mysterious shaman was nowhere to be found.

That evening, after we finished our group dinner, I joined the others at an outside bar that was poolside at our modest accommodations. I inquired of several of the young Mexican tour guides about my mysterious shaman. No one really knew who he was. I felt hopeless. I could not seem to let this go.

The conference culminated in a ceremony on the fall equinox at a Mayan ruin known as Uxmal. As the group marched in quiet procession toward the Pyramid of the Magician, we saw a figure at the center, seated in lotus position in a doorway. There he was! The mysterious shaman, his long black hair blowing in the wind; he must have been sitting about a hundred feet up, looking down upon us. I swear that I could "feel" him. He stayed there until we finished a ceremony in front of the pyramid, then he descended to join us.

Again that little voice commanded, "Do not approach him yet!" Now I was frustrated, but I obeyed and continued on with the group into an area known as the Nunnery Quadrangle. Here we formed a great circle and joined hands in ceremony once again. I was in bliss, our group was bonding, we were all family, and this felt like a mystical reunion.

I was one of the last to leave the Nunnery through a very interesting pyramid-shaped doorway. As I exited the doorway, there to my right was my shaman. It was as if he was waiting for me. He was alone. I approached him and did not speak; he gazed deep into my eyes and began to speak in Spanish. I could make out a few of the words, but it was not what I was hearing, it was more what I was feeling that impacted me the most. I felt the sun and the moon merge inside my body! My arms began to move like they were serpents. There was an exchange of energy between us that left us both vibrating uncontrollably.

We embraced in silence and continued on. I followed him to a small area away from the large group—many witnessing my experience joined us. The shaman and I did not speak, we did not need words, we were telepathically communicating. I was in an altered state of mind; it was as if my spirit had taken over and I knew exactly what to do. He placed me first on the rock at exactly noon and performed a ritual to open my "energy centers." I could not leave the rock—it was like it became a magnet. My butt was stuck to that rock! I remember the shaman claiming it was magic and laughing at me. It was weird!

After this ritual, several others followed. I felt the sun penetrating my entire being and was given guidance to lay flat, arms stretched outward on the earth. I experienced a deep love for mother earth as I penetrated her with this sun energy that had entered me.

The shaman and I proceeded together, with another woman named Kristal, to join the group from the Prophets Conference. They had formed one large circle and an inner small circle with the teachers and elders. There the shaman entered the small circle and waved to me to join him. I was hesitant, as I did not feel that I should be in the "inner" circle. Yet spirit took over, and from that point on I felt as if I had done this before. It was absolutely right that I had come to Mexico. I had been led there for this very reason. At that moment it felt that I was exactly where I was supposed to be, as if the Universe had called me to action. Kristal was on the other side of the shaman, and I sensed that we were anchoring the power of the solar and lunar energy within the circle.

The shaman led a beautiful and energetic ceremony. We breathed together as a group, repeated mantras, and united in a pulsing group heart. At one point, I felt the entire sky open up— as if an interdimensional portal had been opened and I could see the heavens smiling down upon us. The feeling was an extraordinarily vast sense of connection between all life and the universe. It was as if our work in this ceremony had been destined since the beginning of time and we were reuniting to complete it before the new millennium. In this expanded state of awareness I think I finally understood the meaning of "We are all one." It was exhilarating and humbling, joyous and sacred. It was and, to this day, still is one of the most profound experiences of my life.

THE WRONG PUB AT THE RIGHT TIME

★

Kathleen McGowan

The lure of the Emerald Isle is as ancient as it is powerful. In this country filled with mystics and poets since the dawn of time, the very earth radiates mystery and promise to the traveler. An ancient proverb claims that "one cannot visit Ireland a single time; once it is experienced, the soul will yearn for it again and again."

I realized the truth of this age-old wisdom as a teenager, when my grandparents took me to Ireland as a high school graduation gift. True to the proverb, I could not stay away and spent many of my waking hours in America planning the next visit to my ancestral homeland. In the summer of 1984, I had saved enough money to take six months off of work. Along with Della, my best friend from childhood, I set off for Ireland. We were twenty-one years old and hungry to explore and experience every inch of this magical land.

We found ourselves a magnificent residence in Rathmines, a Dublin suburb, to act as our home base. The converted attic of a large Victorian house, it was now a two-bedroom flat, a mass of angles, beams, and skylights. It was only one of the many treasures we would uncover that summer, as we explored and studied and sang Irish ballads with newfound friends all over the country.

Leaving Ireland is always hard for me, and tears rolled down my cheeks as the plane taxied down the runway on its way to America. "The soul will yearn for it again and again" played the proverb in my head as I watched the spectacular coastline fade from view. But I knew I would be back, sooner rather than later.

There was something calling me here, I had felt the first moment I set foot in this extraordinary place.

Two years later, the siren song was too loud to ignore. I succumbed and got on the phone to my former landlady in Dublin. My old flat was currently vacant! For a small deposit, she would hold it for the summer. Della, not one to be excluded from any adventure, signed on to join me for another summer in Ireland. She, too, held a deep love for this land and its people and felt the need to return.

The day we arrived in Ireland was a traveler's nightmare. It was a marathon of waiting: hours at the airport, hours at the train station, hours on the train, and finally the taxi that would take us home to Rathmines. Della and I lugged our rather extensive baggage up the three flights of stairs to our attic home and collapsed. We were both exhausted after our extremely long and tedious journey. But I was overjoyed at the sight of our beloved flat. As I wandered through the rooms, I began to feel totally exhilarated.

"Let's go out," I recommended suddenly.

Della looked at me as if I had completely lost my mind or had suggested we dance naked on the rooftops. "Are you nuts? Aren't you exhausted?"

I couldn't explain it, I hadn't slept in two days and had just traveled over six thousand miles, but suddenly I was all energy. I pleaded with her to come out with me. There was a great pub in Rathmines where we had spent a lot of time meeting the locals during our previous visit. I was dying to go back there, right now, just to feel like I was home.

Della felt it too; I could see it in her face. Something was waiting for us out in the Irish night. We bathed quickly and set out on foot. As we turned on to the Rathmines Road, we passed a small, dark pub that had been there for over a hundred years. I stopped as we walked passed the door, and Della looked at me quizzically.

"Let's go in here," I said suddenly.

Della looked at me again as if I were walking the brink of madness. We had never been in that pub before. The whole point of going out tonight was to visit our favorite local hangout. Besides, this place looked a bit dingy, even scary. Our pub was bright and new and filled with young people. Why would we possibly want to go into this place?

I would not be swayed. I *had* to go into this pub. Della, exhausted beyond argument, accompanied me through the battered wooden door.

Inside, the place wasn't scary at all. It was, in fact, cozy, but certainly quiet compared to our regular haunt. After a few minutes, a waitress came by with two glasses of Irish lager. She pointed to the back of the bar and told us that two young men over there had bought our drinks. We hadn't even noticed them, but now we waved our thanks and smiled back. We were both too tired for small talk, but guilt got the better of me and I finally ventured over to thank them for their gesture.

Both men were Irish, handsome, and in their early twenties. They introduced themselves as Peter and Kevin, and I talked to them for a few minutes. Charming in a way that is specific to Irish men, they said they were musicians and played in a local band, then invited us to come and see them sometime. I told them we would be in Dublin for several months and would be looking for things to do at night, so we might see them again. I thanked them once more and returned to Della. We left shortly after that, giving in to the need for sleep.

Although Dublin is one of the great European capitals, its suburbs have a very small-town feel. We ended up bumping into Peter and Kevin on several occasions after that: at the Laundromat, the grocery store, or just walking down the street. On the last occasion, Peter told us they were playing in town that night and invited us to come to the show. We went, and the world changed after that.

From that night forward the four of us became inseparable. We double-dated for the remaining months we were in Dublin. When the time came for us to return to the States, I sobbed my heart out. Now I was leaving not only my beloved Ireland but Peter as well.

That Christmas, Della and I received gifts: Peter and Kevin arrived in Los Angeles to visit us. On that day Peter and I vowed that we would never be apart again. I married him in his hometown in County Cavan in 1988, and we have two perfectly glorious sons, Patrick and Conor. We live in Los Angeles, but we go "home" as often as we can to see his family.

Della and Kevin were also married, on the Valentine's Day following Kevin's arrival in Los Angeles. They have since returned to Dublin, where they live with their two beautiful little boys, Ian and Declan.

They live only a short distance from that aged little pub with the battered wooden door that called to us on an Irish night, one very special summer.

THE WAKE-UP CALL

★

Donna LeBlanc, M.Ed., D.A.P.A.

The trip to Egypt came from a flyer. That trip is too big for me, I thought. I could never get together that much money. I can't go halfway around the world with a group of people I don't know. But a nudging from inside would not let me turn back. Without knowing why, I decided to go.

After I'd put an ocean between my comfort zone and me, it didn't take long for my insecurities—core beliefs that were running my life, fears I never dreamed I had—to surface. The worst of all: low self-esteem. Oh, no. I was in the business of helping people raise their self-esteem and I wasn't feeling like I had much. Now I could see that my profession was where I had been getting mine; it wasn't present in every cell of my body.

Little did I know that this new awareness, as big as it was, was only the beginning. It would be while lying in a sarcophagus inside the belly of a pyramid that I would face my demons head-on, with no place to hide. The enigmatic chamber of an ancient crypt was to be the place of my "rebirth," shattering my reality and causing an awakening that would change the course of my life forever.

In a state of great anticipation, we twelve spiritual seekers stepped off the bus in front of the larger-than-life pyramid on the Giza plateau. The surreal landscape was peppered with chestnut-colored people on camel back, whose skin had been worn dry from the heat of an unrelenting sun. The great monolithic structure rose out of the sand like an extraterrestrial towering over our lumbering, tired tour bus, dwarfing us in its shadow. Millions of tons of stone blocks, meticulously chiseled by the blood and sweat of our ancestors, formed a stairway into the heavens. It had broad stones at its base on all sides; at the sky it seemed to narrow to a singular step-off point. The crypt held within was supposedly a room unlike any other. Mysterious. Buried deep in the mythology of an ancient culture in this faraway land, surrounded by gusting, parched winds, bleached-bone desert sand, and bright, pale skies as far as the eye could see.

Weak-kneed, I put myself in the back of the line of our small band of explorers in order to conceal the claustrophobia that had been a secret companion all of my life. Only the previous year the problem had caused an embarrassing scene on my first journey to New York. Going to meet editors at a major publishing house, I froze and was unable to get on an elevator; it felt as though there were no breathing room to spare. This episode would dwarf that one—by far.

I was unable to postpone the inevitable; my turn arrived to descend into the crawl space. Four feet in diameter, the tunnel descended for two hundred feet. The gloomy entrance foreshadowed my desperation. Moving into the pit of unexplored darkness below, I felt the separation from my lifeline, the sunlight above. My eyes were wide, my chest heaved; each breath was stolen from beneath the vise tightening around my rib cage. I crouched and felt alone like never before—although I was being coached by one of my companions, who was sensitive enough to feel the crisis at hand. My weathered tennis shoes reached anxiously for the planks of the wooden platform underfoot. The tunnel lacked ventilation, and the air hung with the stale smell of urine and human body odor. The rugged alabaster and smoke-colored crawl space was clogged with those who preceded me. Nonetheless, I was determined not to let the rest of my companions come to know me as weak. I pushed on, frightened and unable to shake a sense of doom, as if I were being buried alive.

Finally, we reached the opening to the crypt of the pyramid. This tomb was an unlit, dismal room, fifteen feet square, with craggy, gray chalk-and-mud walls and an arched ceiling. The damp, cool air hung as if in suspended animation, a vacuum of deadly silence. Small flashlights cast shadows on the walls. At one end I perceived a coal black granite sarcophagus with a heavy, thick lid leaning to one side in the dust and silt.

I clung to the wall, grateful for my survival, to let my breathing calm, while one of our troop climbed inside the sarcophagus.
Then, with reverence and humility, each of the others solemnly
took a turn inside. We were conscious of the fact that this had
been the resting place of an earlier inhabitant for thousands of
years and did not want to defame or disrespect the gift we had
all been given of being able to experience this amazing burial
place without the dirge of other tourists.

My turn arrived too soon. Pensively climbing in, I lay down
and instinctively crossed my arms over my chest—as was the
custom in burials of that period. One of our group leaders began
singing a Gregorian chant. His magnificent voice filled the space
with sounds reminiscent of monks I had heard in monasteries.
The others chimed in, and the room filled with the melodic
sounds of what seemed like ancient times. The acoustics enveloped me and, as if entranced by some mysterious form of
magic, my body felt locked in and immobilized while my soul
was transported to another place and era.

I had died and this was my funeral. These voices were my
family and friends as they sang the beautiful but melancholic
song of good-bye over my body. My fear gave way to grief, and
my soul mourned as I was swept away into the experience. In the
sarcophagus, my body convulsed with waves of emotion and
tears as my life began flashing before my eyes. The experience
felt similar to what is reported by those with near-death experiences. From this viewing point I could clearly see that I had not
been living at all. I had spent twenty years in front of a television
set on my off time and had filled the rest of my days with work.
Even though my body had spent many years inside relationships,
my soul had been tucked safely inside, where no one could hurt
me. Wounded, I was too afraid to really love or take risks.

As I continued weeping and the melodic voices held the space
for my release, my spirit screamed inside my head, "I don't want
to die; I haven't really lived!" I was locked into a nightmare,
while the unrelenting review continued. Next, I saw the dreams
I had told myself I would accomplish one day and never had; the
playing I had not done; all the things I never did but promised
myself I would; the time spent with the same people day in and

day out; the boredom of the past many years; never doing anything that made me afraid, insecure, unsure, or challenged. I realized, for the first time, that I didn't know as much as I thought
I did; that I had been living inside a picture of reality that I had
painted for myself; and, ultimately, that I had been emotionally,
spiritually, and physically dead for many years, even though I
had been hiding safely behind the masks I wore for the world. I
had played many roles with adept skill. My comfort zones were
literally choking the life out of me.

After my identity shattered, my mind was reeling from the
magnitude of the revelations. Tears continued to flow. One of
the group leaders realized the depth of my pain and climbed in
with me. He wrapped his arms around me and began rocking me
like a baby. His compassion, and the human touch, brought me
gratefully back from the edge, and my emotions began to calm.

When I climbed out, I felt as though I were a new person, one
who was awake in a way I had never before imagined. I had been
"born again" into a new life. I was free and alive with a new
commitment to live fully. I had faced my death, and now I understood that the greatest pain comes from the life unlived, not
by staying safe.

Leaving the chamber was like night and day. My chest expanded; the walls felt like Colorado snowbanks. For two hours
afterward, it felt as though ants were crawling under my skin all
over my body, and rushes of energy flushed through my entire
being.

The next night we went to the Great Pyramid, where climbing in was welcoming and warm. My claustrophobia had completely subsided. We crawled down into the Queen's Chamber, a
room shaped like a womb. I waited for the rest of the group to
leave and lingered behind, intuitively knowing some other experience awaited me.

Once alone, I became aware of a spiritual presence. It was as
if a great, universal mother and father spirit were outside and I
was safely inside the womb of the mother. I heard their loving
words: "Donna, this time when you come out, we want you to
really live. Donna, live!" I felt an infusion of love, as though I
were a small child being initiated into this life freshly, with an-

other chance to start. I had permission to live my life for the first time. Having been in the womb of the mother, I felt like I was coming down the canal to my new life. Only this time I would really live!

Now, in a visceral way, I felt the meaning of a message that had come to me through automatic writing some years earlier. At that time, I had been lost in my own maze, moving from one therapist to another without any real change. Then I started meditating frequently, and on some nights an overwhelming drive to write in my journal would come to me. These entries were always written as letters to Donna, as if some benevolent force, or perhaps my higher self, were using the openness of that time to give me most-needed guidance.

On one such night, my hand wrote propelled by an energy all its own. "If your mother and father of blood cannot give you what you need on this earth plane, it is available to you on the other side of the veil and can be channeled to you directly and through healers that can channel the great mother and father energies. These energies can wrap around you and bring you into wholeness so you can set your earthly parents free and feel full of the love and nurturing you need."

There in the Great Pyramid, I truly felt filled with the love of these energies and a freedom from an emptiness that had been with me my whole life. It was being filled with this love that was the beginning of true self-love. I returned to Dallas a new person, seeing my daily life in a completely new way. The changes took time, but I turned off the TV. In the following months I closed my practice in Dallas, moved to New York, and made all new friends who were in alignment with my spiritual growth.

Since the Egypt trip, I have traveled to sacred sites in England, Tibet, India, Nepal, and Bali. I have changed as though I have died and been reincarnated, without having to leave my body. Now I see my life as an ongoing process of revelation, in which I am learning to love, share myself, and give my gifts to the world.

BABA BAKALA: A GLIMPSE OF THE DIVINE

★

Dharma Singh Khalsa, M.D.

Guru Har Krishan, the eighth leader of the Sikh religion, was only nine years old when he left his physical body for the heavenly abode. Just after becoming guru, at age eight, he helped save Delhi, the capital city of India, from the plague. Miraculously, he turned a small body of water into a sacred healing pond, which he then used to cure the sick. Picking up the karmas of the afflicted, and feeling his Creator's call, he succumbed to the illness.

Soothed in silk, and with the scent of sandalwood in the air, his disciples gathered around the young guru. One of his followers, dressed in pure white *bana,* a traditional Indian outfit including a turban, asked in hushed tones, "Oh beloved one, who will be the next true guru?" Guru Har Krishan brought his followers close and, before breathing his last, uttered two words: "Baba Bakala." This meant the next guru was in Bakala, a small village in the Punjab region of Northern India.

Politics being what they are, even in ancient India, twenty-two false prophets set themselves up as the guru in the town of Bakala. They accepted offerings from potential followers and readily blessed them with disingenuous words.

A month later a merchant named Makhan Shah came to Bakala with an offering of five hundred gold coins, which, in prayer, he had vowed to give the guru on escaping a shipwreck. Imagine his surprise when he found that twenty-two men had installed themselves as guru. In this state of confusion and uncertainty, he resolved to make trial of the pretenders. He visited them all, and made them offerings of two gold coins each. None of them knew that he had brought five hundred gold coins for the real guru. Each of them extolled himself and said the others were hypocrites and deceivers.

Realizing all were false, Shah asked the town elders if there was perhaps another holy man. He was directed to the home of Teg Bahadur, who had been in deep meditation on God for twenty-seven years in the small basement of his home.

The sea merchant bowed before Teg Bahadur and placed two gold coins at his feet. "Where are the five hundred you promised when your vessel was sinking?" asked the saint. Makhan Shah shouted with joy, for at last he knew that he had found the next guru.

Against this backdrop I arrived on the Indian subcontinent in November 1997, and after visiting the Golden Temple in Amritsar came to the dusty little village of Bakala with a group of fellow pilgrims. With only two main streets, curbside vendors, and a rugged appearance, the town reminded me of America's Old West. Our Indian tour guide was a thin yet obviously strong Nihung Sikh, or warrior class descendant. He dressed in full blue *bana*. What made him particularly striking, however, was his tall turban, surrounded by thin circular steel ornaments, which could be used for protection against an enemy's sword. Sikhs are well known to be fierce fighters, having not only defended India against the invading Moguls in ancient times but also defeated the Japanese in Burma during World War II. Our guide certainly looked the part. Like many Nihungs, he appeared quite formidable, especially because he carried a long dagger, called a *kirpan*, in his belt.

In Bakala there is a temple or *Gudwara* constructed in honor of Guru Teg Bahadur. After touring the temple, which surrounds the basement opening where he meditated, the group went outside to hear our guide tell us the story. "Guruji sat in that spot and meditated on the glorious name of God for twenty-seven years before he became guru," our guide said.

I raised my hand and asked, "What mantra did he use?" An enraged look came over the face of our guide. "Get out, get out!" he shouted. "You don't believe it!" Apparently he thought I doubted him, which would be very disrespectful. "No, I was just trying to learn the mantra," I stammered, in an effort to explain. "Get out, get out!" He was literally screaming at me now.

Not wanting to incur the wrath of this gentleman, I got up and walked back into the temple. Taking the side entrance, I found myself at a location exactly opposite the open door leading down to the basement room where the guru had meditated on the Nam, the essence of the one creative God. Placing my back against the wall of the temple, I sat and gazed deeply into the depths of the holy den.

At that exact moment, nine words came to my mind in a language I don't speak. *"Dhan Dhan Guru Teg Bahadur Sahibji, Wha Hey Guru."* Translated this means "Honored and adorned is Guru Teg Bahadur, ecstasy is in the light of God." I went immediately into the yogic state of samadhi, at once at one with the entire cosmos. A golden ray of light ran up my spine as new words came. *"Har, Har, Wha Hey Guru"* echoed through my heart and soul. "God's name takes you from darkness to light."

I had no sense of time passing. My breathing slowed and was suspended. The only feeling I had was a mild current of electricity running up my spine and out of the top of my head. In retrospect, it seems as if I was consciously observing myself from outside my being. I became one with the One.

After what seemed like only a moment, I felt the presence of my wife, Kirti, so I slowly opened my eyes and oriented back to earth. She smiled gently at me and whispered that the bus was getting ready to leave and I was missed. I had been meditating for close to an hour, she said. Bowing to the guru, we walked out into the hot, bright sun and boarded the bus.

Guru Teg Bahadur gave me the gift of his mantra. This great man, who years later gave his life to defend the freedom of everyone to worship God as they wished, and whose son, Guru Gobind Singh, created the brotherhood of the Khalsa, that day became my spiritual grandfather.

It is written in the Siri Guru Granth Sahib, the divine hymns of the Sikhs, "Meditate on Guru Teg Bahadur and the nine treasures shall run to your door." Experiencing His power, I learned that meditating on God in the company of holy like-minded people and tuning in to His will can bring you all the beauty that life has to offer. The distance between yourself as you are at the moment and your true divine essence will shorten. More than that, I confirmed that exalted consciousness can come through commitment to a daily spiritual practice, and that God is realized in the simple kindness shown in everyday behavior.

May contentment reign within your heart, and may our world be blessed with peace. *Sat Nam.*

MY SOUL RETRIEVAL

Irina H. Corten Ph.D.

It was a snowy January afternoon in 1995. I was visiting a friend, Rose, who is a holistic healer. Warming ourselves by the fireplace, we began to talk about our childhood memories. Mine were not happy ones. I spent my early years in Russia when it was still under the tyrannical regime of Joseph Stalin. Although my family was loving and supportive, I suffered from the authoritarian methods practiced at school and from the general atmosphere of fear and oppression that pervaded the country. These experiences had left deep emotional scars.

Having listened to my grim stories, Rose said, "I think you could benefit from a soul retrieval." Seeing my baffled look, she explained that soul retrieval is a healing method used in shamanism. It is intended for people who, as a result of some physical or emotional trauma, lose part of their spiritual selves; in other words, their souls become fragmented. The belief is that, in order to escape the trauma, a part of one's soul splits off and moves into a multidimensional realm called nonordinary reality. This leaves the person in a weakened and dispirited condition, and it is the task of the shamanic healer to restore wholeness. The healer goes on a visionary journey into nonordinary reality (otherwise known as the shamanic journey) and, with the help of spirit guides, tracks down the soul fragment and brings it back to the patient.

The soul retrieval method sounded intriguing, and I wanted to hear more about it and shamanism in general. Rose said that shamanism is a spiritual discipline that requires years of study and practice to master, although basic shamanic methods can be learned relatively quickly and applied effectively if one has a penchant for them. A shaman, she said, is a person who enters an altered state of consciousness—at will—to contact an ordinarily hidden reality in order to obtain knowledge, power, and healing. Shamanism is the world's oldest spiritual tradition and has been practiced for thousands of years. Although there are variations in shamanic rituals from culture to culture, the underlying principle of the visionary journey is shared and adaptable to the needs of modern society. Shamanism is a holistic practice that enables us to live in greater harmony with our environment. It is a source of knowledge of the vast and fascinating world that lies beyond the limits of our rational mind and three-dimensional perception.

I decided to have a soul retrieval and returned to Rose's house several days later, feeling excited and a bit nervous. Before we began, Rose spoke about the importance of the drum in shamanic journeying. The steady, rhythmic beat of the drum enables the journeyer to enter a relaxed and expanded state of consciousness. Ideally, there should be live drumming, but in its absence one can listen to a recording. Rose also explained that, in working with me, she would deviate somewhat from standard practice. Typically, when a shaman journeys on behalf of a client, the client lies passively waiting for the shaman to bring back the soul part and blow it into the client's body. Knowing my strong interest in things metaphysical, however, Rose decided to have me do a parallel journey of my own.

In shamanic cosmology, nonordinary reality is divided into three realms: the Lower, the Upper, and the Middle Worlds. The Lower World is accessed through an opening such as a tree hollow, a crater, a water hole, or any other natural conduit leading downward into the earth. The Upper World may be reached by going up a rainbow, up a column of smoke, or on the wings of a flying bird. The Middle World is entered horizontally through a bank of fog, a thicket of leaves, or some other type of natural membrane. An experienced shaman knows intuitively which of these locations is the most suitable for the task at hand. Beginners usually go into the Lower World, as it seems to be the easiest one for most people to visualize. In every one of these domains there are landscapes, objects, and entities waiting to teach and to help us. Information is given either in words or through symbolic images.

Rose and I lay down on the floor next to each other in a darkened room, covered our eyes, and began listening to a CD recording of shamanic drums. With some trepidation, I visualized jumping down a tree hollow. The following sequence of events was completely unexpected and had the quality of lucid dreaming with perfect recall.

I saw myself going through a long, foggy tunnel that eventually brought me to the playground outside our apartment building in Moscow. I saw myself as a child of about nine. It was twilight, and no one was there. I felt disoriented and driven by an urgent need to find something or someone. I looked up at the sky and saw a huge, illumined visage of Stalin floating through the air. This image was based on ordinary reality. On December 21, 1949, Stalin's seventieth birthday was celebrated with a lot of fanfare, and blimps carried his lighted portrait over Moscow at night. I was very impressed with that spectacle as a child.

In my shamanic vision, Stalin's image expanded, descended from the sky, and enveloped me with a thick, cold mist. His presence felt masculine and paternal but at the same time frightening and evil, almost diabolic. I cried out for help, whereupon a beautiful black mountain goat with long, silky hair and golden eyes materialized and came toward me. I slipped under her belly, hid behind her udders and thick hair, and she carried me safely out of the Stalin cloud. She told me to call her Mother Goat.

Next we went to my school, which was nearby. The building was empty. I went through its corridors looking for my soul, and finally saw it under the ceiling of my classroom. It looked like a long, pale blue ribbon of energy, a kind of spectral snake. Realizing that I was looking at it, it zigzagged swiftly through the air, drifted out of the window, and disappeared. Then Mother Goat and I left the school, crossed the yard, and came up to the steps of a Russian Orthodox church.

There was an old crone sitting on the steps of the church. She called me and said I had to go with her. I was aware of some danger in this situation, but it seemed important that I accept the challenge. Mother Goat was by my side, and I knew she would protect me. The old crone took me to her village deep in the wooded countryside. The time dimension was a mythic past of

Russian fairy tales. I saw myself as a little peasant girl in a shabby, long dress and babushka scarf of nondescript color. I played for a while in the old woman's garden and then wandered off into the woods, followed by Mother Goat.

Suddenly I saw my soul again. This time it appeared in the form of a little peasant girl identical to me in age and appearance, only her clothes were new and pretty and her babushka scarf was bright blue. She was as confident and playful as I was confused and sad. She laughed and frolicked and teased me, running among the trees at a distance. I realized that she was luring me deeper into the woods, and I followed her. Finally we came to a clearing where a tall bonfire was blazing. The little girl began to dance around the fire and finally merged with it, her body transforming itself into long, ribbonlike shapes of vertical flames. For a fleeting instant I saw her in the flames as a huge goddesslike entity. Then the fire went out, and I saw Mother Goat standing over the ashes with the girl sitting on her back. The animal leapt up and galloped joyfully off into the sky, carrying the laughing child with her.

The concluding episode of my soul journey had the quality of a cosmic teaching. My consciousness hugely expanding, I saw the entire landscape of the earlier scenes: my house, yard, school, church, village, woods, and forest glade. Underneath this landscape there was a vast network of subterranean tunnels. Snakelike energy ribbons, similar to the ones I saw in the classroom and in the bonfire, danced energetically in the air before my eyes. Then, like powerful electrical shock waves, these ribbons zoomed through the entire landscape, penetrating and connecting everything and showing me that it was all One.

The drum stopped, I opened my eyes and said, *"Wow! Incredible!"* I began to sit up, but Rose pushed me down with great urgency, telling me to lie still. She then blew several forceful breaths into my chest and the crown of my head. She was using the shamanic technique of blowing a retrieved soul part into the patient's body. A few minutes later she helped me sit up and described her own journey:

"My power animal—a flying horse—came to me, I mounted it, and we rode off into the Upper World. There was a portal, and on the other side of it we were met by my guide, a wise old man in a black, pointed hat. He gave me a large box, saying that it contained important and valuable things, but I was not to look at them. Riding further, I came face to face with a very powerful and malicious spirit, a human male entity with large whiskers. He blocked my way, but I held out the box to him and said he could open it and take anything he liked. He did, and let me ride further.

"The horse carried me to a very far region of space. I saw a lush garden encircled by a fence. It was full of children's souls. They seemed happy enough but were unable to leave the enclosure. They were tended by small silvery-colored beings with circular heads. I saw your soul—a pale little girl with large, clear eyes—peering out from behind the others. She seemed interested in going with me, but the beings told me she was happy with them and would not let her go. I held out the box to them. They extracted something from it and released your soul to me.

"As we began to descend, I realized that the silvery beings had changed their minds, and were pursuing us to take you back. I spurred the horse with all my power, and we barely made it here in time for me to blow your soul into your body."

This soul retrieval was a big turning point in my life. It enabled me to make contact with the "lost child" aspect of myself. Initially I was unable to fully grasp the symbolism of the journeys, but eventually it became clear and explained many problems that had been plaguing me from childhood. I became extremely interested in shamanism and have been studying and practicing it ever since. I learned that shamanic journeys are undertaken not only for the purpose of soul retrieval but also for obtaining answers to a wide variety of questions, ranging from profoundly serious to relatively mundane, such as how to cope with cold winters. Mother Goat and my alter ego—the little girl in a blue babushka, whom I now call Fire Child—have been my teachers and frequent companions in other journeys.

Although I still have much to learn about shamanism, I have started to do journeys and other types of shamanic healings on behalf of other people. Shamanism teaches one how to be healthy, joyful, and eager to be of service to others, and I am infinitely grateful to Spirit for having led me to this path.

MEDUGORJE MATERIALIZATION

★

Iris Freelander, D.D.

The Blessed Mother had been appearing to the six children in Medugorje, Yugoslavia, for six years before I heard of the unusual happening. At one of my regularly scheduled Wednesday evening church services, I outlined the information that I had read regarding her appearances to children at Fatima, Garabandal, Lourdes, Beauraing, and Zeitoun. A young man in the audience asked, "Have you heard that She has been appearing to children in Yugoslavia? *60 Minutes* had a brief note of that."

My enthusiastic response was a quick "No, but if anyone has further information will you please let me know?" Consequently, I received a note in the mail describing a book by the Reverend Joseph A. Pelletier, A.A., *The Queen of Peace Visits Medugorje,* available at the Center for Peace in Boston, Massachusetts. My order for that fascinating book was immediately put in the mail, together with the request that my name be put on any Medugorje-involved West Coast mailing list.

On a Friday very soon after that, I received notice in the mail of a tour generated by a local travel company that was to leave LAX the following Monday morning. Together with fourteen other eager participants, that Monday morning, with high expectations, I was on a plane en route to Medugorje. The actual events far exceeded my expectations.

I was thrilled by several mystical experiences while there, but the one I now relate to you was perhaps the most significant. At Medugorje, in addition to the Church of Saint James, there are two places of greatest renown. Adjacent to the church is Apparition Hill on Mount Podbrdo, where the Blessed Mother first appeared to some of the six children. At the top of the mile-high Mount Krizevac, the Mountain of the Cross, stands a fifteen-ton concrete cross, which was erected by the people of the area to commemorate the nineteenth centenary of the Redemption. All material used in the construction was carried by hand up the 1,770-foot-high mountain.

The tour group with whom I traveled had gone to Medugorje for a one-week stay, but I had made arrangements to be there for two weeks, encompassing Palm Sunday, my birthday, and Easter Sunday.

On my birthday, March 29, 1988, I walked alone to Apparition Hill. Many other pilgrims were chanting the rosary at the various crosses, particularly at the primary cross, which was said to mark the spot where the Blessed Mother first appeared to some of the children. I circled the area, looking for a flat stone on which to sit for my time of special meditation. At a point about halfway around the circle, my hands were feeling cold. Although I had worn warm jogging apparel, I was fondly remembering the warm gloves left in my cottage.

As I paused and looked at the ground, a single glove beckoned to me. As it slipped easily over my hand, I was thinking that it would at least keep one hand warm while the other could be warmed in my jogging suit pocket. But I heard my inner voice say, "Put it back," and I dutifully complied. I walked another quarter round of the circle before finding a spot to sit and meditate, with a large, flat stone the perfect seating arrangement. The sunlight streamed onto the cleared area, giving impetus to my rewarding time of meditation. For quite some time, I sat there enjoying the vibrant energy generated by the group, and perhaps also residual energy, plus my own silence and connection to Divine Reality. It was a perfect birthday meditation.

Joyously, I rose to leave the area. Glancing at the ground beside me, I became incredulous. Involuntarily I sat back down. Imagine my amazement to have seen a pair of gloves lying right there. After regaining my breath I tried them on. A perfect fit.

I sat quietly in the bright sunlight, serene and content, not only from my wonderfully rewarding meditation but also from the amazingly delightful surprise gift of warm gloves. My gratitude to Creator God for His beneficent love was and remains boundless. The memory will be with me always. So will the gloves. While wholeheartedly treasuring them, I have worn them many times. There have also been times when I have allowed friends to wear those magical gloves. Who knows what healing they might impart? To me, those wondrous gloves are the spirit of Medugorje. Allowed to bring them back to my home, I was given a priceless souvenir.

I WILL NEVER FORGET

★

Elizabeth Seely

On the spur of the moment, I decided to spend Easter in England with my relatives. I quickly rummaged through the top dresser drawer looking for anything I might need on my five-day excursion. Along with some makeup, a few photographs, and a magazine, I threw a pocket-size German dictionary into my duffel bag. I stopped for a moment to contemplate if it was really necessary. I was merely going to England. The dictionary would be no use to me, unless of course I was to meet someone who spoke German.

I thought about my one holiday to Germany twenty years earlier. It was the summer of 1977, and I was fifteen years old. My oldest sister, Carolyn, was accompanying her husband on a business trip to Europe. He would be attending seminars in Germany, and they also planned to travel through France and England. Their only dilemma was needing child care for their two little boys. I jumped at the offer to join them and relished the opportunity. Consequently, I joined my sister and her family in Chicago, and the five of us then flew to Frankfurt. My mother had purchased the little German dictionary for me.

Our final destination that week was a town by the name of Baden-Baden in southwest Germany. On arrival, I was instantly in awe of this quaint village. Baden-Baden was the epitome of what I imagined Germany to be; like a picture postcard, the inn where we stayed greeted us with bright red geraniums overflowing from baskets hung outside the many-paned windows. The Black Forest encompassed the village from a distance—a sight quite breathtaking for a young American girl on her first trip.

The next day I chose to take my nephews for a walk. We headed toward a nearby hill from which we could see a distant church steeple. The experience felt enchanted. I wondered what it would have been like during World War II, when my father, an American paratrooper, had been serving in Europe. Strangely, at the same time I thought of that long ago war I also felt a profound, lingering sense of serenity.

Now I had to make a decision. I tossed the dictionary back into my drawer. The following day I flew from Columbus, Ohio, to Chicago. I had made flight reservations only two days prior and did so without a current passport. Encouraged by my own optimism, I was determined to obtain a passport in Chicago. Unfortunately, my day did not go as planned. I had difficulty finding the place to return my rental car in Columbus and almost missed my first flight. Then, after an exhausting day in downtown Chicago, my patience was expended. It took hours before I was issued a passport.

With no time to spare, I ditched the round-trip shuttle ticket I had purchased earlier and hailed a taxi. I told the driver to go as fast as possible to the airport. I raced through the airport and, with only minutes to spare, I arrived at the assigned gate. As I stood in line, I quietly sighed with relief. I was finally about to depart on my journey. And with that thought in mind, I slid my hand into the side pocket of my floral green carry-on bag, only to find that my tickets and my just-issued passport were missing . . . gone. A sudden warmth ascended to my cheeks, and I felt anxiety surging over me. In despair, I realized I had lost both my tickets and my passport!

Maybe I was just not meant to get on this flight, I thought. Perhaps the whole trip was not meant to be. Maybe all the day's obstacles had been omens that I should postpone traveling.

My only stop on the way to the international gate had been a brief trip to the rest room. Retracing my steps, I knew that was the only possible place I could have left the tickets. I grabbed my bag and jogged down the long hall to where I had been. But as I approached the door, I saw that the rest room had been closed. "What luck," I groaned. Then I called, "Hello?" hoping that someone was inside. A kind attendant went back into the rest room to look for my lost items and returned momentarily, with tickets and passport in hand. I was so relieved. I thanked her humbly and jogged back down to the gate.

Exhausted, hungry, and a little shaken, I was not receptive when the ticket attendant informed me that my seat number was incorrect. "How can this be? I have had an assigned seat since I purchased my ticket in Columbus," I snapped at him. After all I had been through, I did not want to waive the window seat I had asked for. To my dismay, I had no choice. Somehow the computer system had assigned two people to the same seat. Since I had arrived late, I was going to have to accept a new seat assignment. I boarded the plane feeling like the unluckiest person in the world.

Once settled in, I stretched out and relaxed. I planned to eat dinner quickly and then sleep until landing at Heathrow Airport in London. My only desire was that the passenger not yet seated next to me would not interrupt my intended plans. With that, a tall gentleman about my age came down the aisle and opened the overhead compartment above me. He smiled while placing a black leather jacket and bag next to my belongings and cheerfully said, "Hi, how are you?" I smiled back. It didn't look as if that wish was going to come true.

We chatted. I explained my exhausting day to the stranger seated next to me, while he listened sympathetically. He lived in London and was intending to work in the States. Originally, like myself, he was from Ohio. We compared stories about our children, who were similar ages. Our conversation flowed freely. It was both relaxing and exhilarating at the same time, comparable to running into a longtime friend. He felt like someone I was destined to meet. I started to get excited again about London.

During our flight across the Atlantic, I mentioned to my seatmate that one of my favorite places in the world was a small town in Germany. As I said it I thought about the mystical feeling I had had in Baden-Baden. I thought of the German dictionary I somehow had felt compelled to bring with me although I had resisted the urge.

The gentleman asked enthusiastically, "Where in Germany?"

"Oh, a little place near the Black Forest called Baden-Baden," I responded.

With a surprised and yet knowing look on his face, he said, "I used to visit there often as a boy! My mother is German. She

came to America after World War II, which is how she met my
father, but my grandmother still lives there. I still go there every
six months!"

I felt an immediate connection with this stranger, and I recognized the same feeling that had moved me so deeply when I
was a teenager in Germany twenty years earlier. "Please say
something in German," I pleaded to my new friend. He did, and
we continued to talk through the night until we were interrupted
by the pilot announcing the view in the northern night sky.

We gazed out the left window as a wondrous, shining yellow
light caught our attention. It was the comet Hale-Bopp. Suddenly I remembered reading once that the people of ancient civ-
ilizations felt comets were signs from the gods. Likewise, seeing
the comet, I was inspired by a sense of faith that everything was
as it was meant to be, and I knew powerfully that someday I
would reach the destination intended for me in life, as well as on
this journey.

For some reason, it was at that moment that I turned around
and asked my companion his name.

Blushing, he said, "Luck. My name is Mr. Luck."

III

Dreams
and Visions

GIFTS OF THE GODDESSES

Arielle Ford

One of my favorite weekend getaways with my husband, Brian, is Esalen in Big Sur, California. It is one of the most beautiful pieces of property in the world and certainly one of the most serene. Known for its hot mineral baths overlooking the Pacific Ocean and for fabulous massages, Esalen also offers transformational seminars of all kinds. This particular July weekend, Brian and I had signed up for a workshop in shamanic journeying. Yet, on the morning we were to begin our three-hour inner journey, I found myself resisting the process.

Even though I had enjoyed journeys in the past, I was particularly resistant to this one because I knew our workshop leader, Jeremiah Abrams, was going to lead us through some very intense breath work. We would be lying on the floor listening to all kinds of rhythmic music and drumming, and being guided to other worlds. My body was tense, and I didn't want to lie on the floor for that long; I couldn't get comfortable.

In spite of my initial resistance, I found that the breathing and the drumming swept me along to another world—an inner dimension that I had never experienced previously. In the first scene I saw Ammachi, my spiritual teacher, who is considered a living saint in India. Ammachi was holding a candle and blessing me. Then I looked around and saw hundreds or thousands of other women holding candles, and all of them seemed to be blessing me as well.

At one point I noticed a wooden fence that looked brand-new. It was in the shape of a square and surrounded what I knew to be my future—a future that would come to pass that fall. Although on one level I wanted to know what was behind the fence, on another level I knew that I wasn't supposed to see any of it. A little voice said to me, "There is no master plan; it's always about choice." The voice also gave me a solution to a business problem that I had been thinking about.

In the next scene I was inside a beautiful cathedral resembling Notre-Dame. I was dressed in a gorgeous off-white wedding gown of antique lace with a high neck, long sleeves, a fitted bodice, and a very long train. I was carrying a bouquet of yellow buttercups and lilies of the valley. But when I looked around for the groom, I did not see one. There was just me, walking down the aisle toward the altar.

As I approached the altar, I found Ammachi sitting in a large thronelike chair. Her radiant smile drew me closer, and I instinctively knew at this moment that I was marrying the Goddess. Ammachi placed a slim gold ring on my left hand.

I became aware that the cathedral had filled with goddesses: Kwan Yin, Isis, Artemis, Aphrodite, Kali, Sekhnet, Mary, Laxshmi, and others. They had each brought me a gift. Laxshmi placed a necklace on me made of huge emeralds that looked like small rocks. Isis showed me that I had wings folded into the back of my wedding dress, and she taught me how to fly. Sekhnet taught me to go within and be very still. Kali taught me to dance wildly and withhold nothing. Artemis explained (as we walked to the top of a mountain) that she helps me in business. Kwan Yin quietly told me that she teaches me patience and compassion. And Mary showed me a past life where I was a young girl who lived during the time of Jesus.

Slowly they all went into my heart, as if they have always lived there. They whispered to me that they are always available to help me . . . all I need to do is ask.

I feel deeply honored to have been given time with the goddesses and to receive their many blessings. I am also grateful for the breath work Jeremiah Abrams taught, which enabled me to overcome my original resistance to make this special journey to a place of illumination. The gifts I received prove to me that we all have the tools at our disposal to connect with a divine experience when we need it. We are born with breath and heart and abilities the goddesses nurture. All we have to do is ask!

A VISIT TO THE
HEAVENLY KITCHEN

★

Sarabeth Archer

I didn't know anything about him apart from the fact that he was damn good looking and teaching something I wanted very much to learn.

His name was Tony, and I found him on a corkboard outside the local supermarket. "Harness your own energy," the small notice declared. "Learn Qigong." When I walked into the room that day at the Y and saw the face behind the claim, I knew I had made the right decision. I wrote out a check, confident that, if nothing more, the twelve weekly sessions in view of that tight butt would improve my energy all on their own.

To my surprise, it was the simplest of techniques, requiring only a modest devotion of my time, and the rewards were apparent immediately. Even after a few classes I was beginning to feel the change in the way energy flowed through me. To my delight, Tony had a terrific personality in addition to looks and a great skill at teaching. Once we added the meditations to the form itself, I felt tension levels melt away from my everyday life. Everyday life back then consisted only of working the counter at a nearby convenience store, but even stocking shelves somehow became easier. The annoyances of curt customers or the nasty comments often lobbed my way by my supervisor seemed less and less effective in touching my daily mood. And all for only thirty minutes of effort each morning and evening.

The class as a whole began to look forward to seeing each other. It felt as if the quality of my social life was improving along with a stronger sense of my own power and a genuine ability to fight off ailments like colds and stomachaches before they

erupted into bigger health problems. Despite having never been
the sort of person who believes in forces greater than my own, I
found that this ancient Chinese art was right up my personal
alley. There was no talk of God; no one was shoving dogma at
me. And no one linked these classes to issues of spirituality or
"otherworldly" events. That's why, when I took my first meditative flight and was given a message from the other side, I was
the first one to disbelieve in what I had actually experienced.

Mind you, Tony had warned us that doing this kind of energy
work might very well connect us to memories we had long ago
repressed. He also hinted at the possibility that some of us might
even have visions of some sort while sitting. I never would have
guessed he was talking to me. Even now, I have no idea why his
younger brother chose me to carry a message to him. But I've
always been very good at doing what I'm told—ask my old boss
at the Stow 'n' Go. Choose me he did.

It might have been because I was also exerting energy trying
to get Tony to go out with me. Nothing dramatic, nothing that
would have sent him running the other way if he weren't interested—just that little extra attention beamed at him while he
talked to me. Hanging around to ask a question or two after
class had broken up. Smiling openly whenever I caught him
looking my way. That sort of thing. It finally paid off when, after
eight or nine classes, he asked me if I might want to have a cup
of coffee with him. Coffee led to coffee again, then lunch, then a
plan to meet for dinner exactly one week before the end of
classes.

The time we spent together was smooth and easy. We talked
about families and favorite movies, old relationships, and new
ways to look at the world that were kinder than some of the
ones we hoped we were beginning to shed. No "date" was long
enough to really plumb the emotional depths, but maybe that
was for the best. I don't know. I didn't know or care about much
beyond the fact that, whether it was Tony's company or the
Qigong, or both, I was feeling better about being me than I had
in years.

I had worked the morning shift at the store, which gave me
at least two hours to get ready for dinner that night. So I decided

to meditate now, in case the evening turned to more immediate gratifications, leaving me no time (or inclination) to stop and sit before going to bed. I did the form, focusing intently on my breathing, feeling my chi begin to pulse in the pit of my abdomen, then moving that throbbing energy to various parts of my body.

Then I sat cross-legged on my little couch pillow inside the slanting box of sunlight streaming through my bedroom window. I don't recall just how long I sat there before I felt myself being pulled away from where I sat and virtually hurtled through space to a bright yellow kitchen I'd never seen before, but suddenly there I was. I could see the bright yellow of the walls, the warm wood floor, and the gleaming white metal cupboards. When I say yellow, I don't refer only to the color of paint: the yellow of this room literally imbued the space. It was the golden yellow of warmth and love—a place of contentedness, a place where I felt instantly welcome.

Outside the single window over the sink I could see a grove of magnificent pine trees. Just as I turned to see what might be behind me, a young boy walked in. He looked to me to be no more than ten, and he was wearing the kind of striped, short-sleeved shirt that was so popular on boys back in the late sixties. Like Opie Taylor used to wear on *The Andy Griffith Show*. In fact, the boy looked very much like Ron Howard did back then: freckled, short-cropped brown hair, and absolutely adorable.

He smiled as he walked up to me. I'm pretty sure I smiled back. He was completely unafraid of me, completely at ease in these surroundings. Without pausing to ask me who I was or why I was in his kitchen, "Opie" said to me, "Tell Tony that everything's okay. Tell him that I am happy and that none of it was his fault. Tell him he needs to go on living and let it go."

And with that, he and the kitchen disappeared, and I was snapped out of my meditation.

At dinner I was distracted over how the hell to bring up the idea of this message to Tony. He talked on about this and that, and I tried to feign interest, all the while debating the validity of what I'd seen and heard. Just how do you bring a message from the dead up in a casual conversation? I thought to myself. And if I do, will I still have a shot at sleeping with this guy? And what would happen to me if I chose *not* to pass along this little boy's simple words?

Whether it was the wine or the instinct I have for doing what I'm told, I blurted out my intro: "Tony, didn't you tell me that you have a brother?"

"That's right."

"But he's still alive, right?"

Tony paused a moment. "Well, Mike, my older brother, is still alive. That's who I told you about. I did have a younger brother, Kevin, who died when he was nine . . . but I don't remember telling you about him."

"Tell me about the house you grew up in," I asked a little too quickly.

"Well—"

"Not the whole house," I said, "just the kitchen."

He eyed the level in my wineglass before saying, "It was this tiny little galleylike room, which was weird because the rest of the house was—"

"What color was it?"

"Color?" He stared at me without blinking. "What's going on?"

"Just humor me," I said, realizing I was in it now, so I'd better just go ahead.

"It was a cream color."

"Not yellow?" I asked.

"No."

"Was there a window over the sink?"

"Yeah, there was," he said, shifting in his seat. "Are you—"

"Were there pine trees outside the window?"

"No. I grew up in the city."

My heart fell. The color and size of the room may not have been just as I remembered seeing them, but there was no mistaking the trees. Majestic, magnificent, deep green pine trees. I swallowed hard, my mind racing over what to say next.

Suddenly Tony said, with genuine animation in his voice, "Wait a minute. There was a house we lived in, but just for a year. It had this fabulous yellow kitchen— God, I haven't thought of that room in years . . ."

I perked up. "And outside the window . . . ?"

He stared at me evenly, seriously. "A grove of pine trees. How the hell did you know that?"

I sat forward in my chair. "Just let me get this out, Tony. I was meditating this afternoon when I was suddenly . . . transported to this yellow kitchen with pine trees outside the window. I met a young boy there. It was funny, my first thought when I saw him was that he looked just like Opie Taylor from Mayberry; do you remember that show? I used to . . . Tony?"

Tony sat motionless on the other side of the candlelit table. Absolutely still. I waited for him to speak.

"My brother Kevin was a dead ringer for Opie on that show. He even used to wear those striped T-shirts all the time. . . ."

I took a deep breath. "Tony, this kid was wearing one of those striped shirts. He walked right up to me and told me to tell you that he's fine, that everything's okay, and that none of it was your fault. He also—"

"*What?*"

"Um, yeah, he said to 'tell Tony that none of it was his fault and that he needs to get over it and start living.' Now, I don't know if what happened was . . . was anything. And if it is a real message, I don't know if I was meant to bring it to you. But since you're the only Tony I know, I figured, well—"

Tony held up a hand for me to stop talking. He took a drink from his water glass and looked down into his lap for a long, long time. When he finally looked up at me, his eyes were wet with tears.

"My brother Kevin died at that house. Out in the backyard. That was why we only lived there a year." He paused, cleared his throat. "He, uh, he died of a blood clot that burst in his brain." Tony breathed in deeply, exhaled slowly. "Man, I haven't ever told anyone this . . ."

"If you don't want to tell me, Tony, it's okay—"

"No. Are you kidding? My kid brother came a long way to talk to you. He obviously trusted you for some reason. Why shouldn't I?" The waiter started toward us with the water pitcher, but Tony waved him off. He leaned forward in his chair and very softly told *me*—a virtual nobody in his life—his deepest secret.

"That day, Kevin had done something that really pissed me off. I can't even remember to this day what it was . . . but I took this little block of wood I was playing with and I . . . I socked him on the head with it.

"He went down, and he did not move. I got so scared. I hauled that chunk of wood over this fence and into a neighbor's yard, and then I ran like hell for my mother. He wasn't even alive by the time we got him to the hospital."

"Wow. That must've been a nightmare for you."

"That's an understatement. The thing was that Kev had fallen a couple of days earlier and cracked his head. Apparently I ended up hitting him right near that same spot—there wasn't any blood or anything, and the bump was already there . . . but in all this time I have not been able to get over believing that I killed my brother. . . . It's actually the reason I got into the meditative martial arts and away from any forms of violence."

"Well," I said, my voice catching a bit in my tight throat, "that was probably a very good thing to have done with your life. But maybe now it's time for you to do it without all that baggage, hell, without that lie hanging over your head . . ." I let my words drift off. I had no idea what else to say.

"Maybe now I can," he added, looking straight at me. "Maybe now I can." He reached his hand across the table, past the candles glowing the same warm, golden light I'd felt and seen in the kitchen.

I smiled warmly as I took Tony's hand in mine, deeply grateful—finally—for being the kind of person who is very good at doing what she's told.

THE FIRST TIME
I SAW THE ANGELS

★

Connie Kaplan

I didn't recognize them at first. The circumstances were so odd that I thought I was having a sunstroke. Let me explain.

Several years before this incident, I had encountered a bizarre disease that basically wiped out my brain. Up until that time I'd been the sort of Type A person who could store and prioritize information without benefit of a notepad, I could make complex choices and discern the consequences of them, I could discriminate between important pieces of information and gibberish. I had a successful career as a television associate director, in which my rather amazing brain capacity was being well used. Then suddenly, one day I didn't feel well, and by the end of the week I couldn't remember my daughter's name, nor could I discern the difference between the doorbell and the telephone.

For the next few years I went through an amazing transformation. I released my former self. I became prolific in the dreaming realms, because all I could really do well was sleep. I learned a lot about dreams in the dreamtime, and eventually began teaching what I had learned to others.

I went to see Beautiful Painted Arrow, a modern mystic, at the suggestion of a friend who told me he could most likely help me understand what had happened to me. In our first private meeting, I began to explain to him one of the recurring dreams of this eighteen-month-long nap I'd taken. This dream involved a teacher who always took me to a specific waterfall in a specific canyon where he would teach me about the unique plants and rocks in that canyon.

Joseph (Beautiful Painted Arrow's Christian name) agitatedly interrupted me and asked how soon I could come to New Mexico. We made a plan for the not-too-distant future. On the designated day I went to his home to visit him. No sooner had I arrived than he said, "Let's go. I have something to show you." We drove almost a hundred miles before he told me to pull over. It reminded me of Carlos Castaneda and his teacher Don Juan's journeys. We stopped the car and abandoned it by the highway. We then walked for almost three hours. And, suddenly, there was my waterfall. *The* very waterfall I'd dreamed dozens of times. I was astonished.

So Beautiful Painted Arrow became my teacher, and I started to piece together, with his help, many of the important teachings I'd received while I slept myself awake!

Two years later he invited me to participate in a ceremonial dance. His vision was that this would be both a dance to the sun (somewhat following the traditional Sun Dance of the Native People) and a moon dance, honoring the power of dreamtime. It was during my first SunMoon Dance that the angels came.

I'd been in the ceremony almost twenty-four hours. It was a hot July, dry New Mexico day. I was lying on my sleeping pad in the corral, sweating profusely, watching the ants crawling all over me, not caring. I'd had no food or water and was acutely aware of the fact that I don't believe one can survive in the heat of the summer without food and water. I looked up at the ceremonial tree and saw two very tall people walking toward me. They were in ceremonial garb with feathers and some sort of back piece that looked almost like wings. I thought they were some of the people guarding the dancers.

One offered me his hand and helped me stand. They asked me to follow them out of the corral. I told them it was against the rules for me to leave the corral without Beautiful Painted Arrow's permission. They put their fingers over their mouths, as if to say, "Don't tell." Being one to break the rules if I thought I could get away with it, I quietly followed them. Amazingly, no one noticed.

They took me down a trail, and we entered an Indian campground from some other century. I thought it marvelous that all these Indians had come and set up an old-style tipi village to support our dance. I then realized something profound—realized the way you realize in a dream without explanation—these people were dead. My guides told me that they had all been wiped out one afternoon in 1860 something. Because they had not been properly grieved (they had no survivors to cry and pray for them), they hadn't moved. They hadn't even realized they were dead. They simply set up camp on the Other Side and ignored their own reality, much the way living people do.

I was jolted then into a two-part consciousness. I saw myself still sitting in the corral at the dance. My physical body hadn't left at all. It was my visionary body that was on this journey. My double? My etheric body? What was it? Who was it on this trip? Was I dead?

My guides took this mysterious me to many other places to introduce me to people who hadn't been grieved. They explained that human prayers are essential to the dead. When the average person dies, he or she needs human prayers and tears to use as the pathway for the soul journey. Without anyone to grieve the death, the average person just stays in a level of consciousness that allows for no movement. What's of even more concern is that they stay close enough to the typical band of human consciousness to maintain a "vote" in the collective attitude. We can do all the work we want in our airy-fairy New Age to "raise our consciousness," but until we release the dead from their stuckness—until we provide the river of prayers and tears on which they can float home—we may as well hang it up. They're outvoting us.

Within a few hours I had met almost two hundred thousand people who were dead and waiting to be grieved. I felt impotent. There was no way I could grieve all these people. The task seemed too much, the burden too heavy. The guides told me to remember what I know, and then returned me to the corral.

I couldn't remember a thing that I knew about death. I had no idea what they meant. Didn't they know that my memory banks had been eaten a few years earlier by some virus? I dissolved into a river of my own tears.

A few days later I was on the road back to Santa Fe. The dance had been over for three days, and I'd driven to Beautiful

Painted Arrow's house to tell him of my visionary experience. On the road back, a man flagged me down. Someone in his car was very ill. It was an old Indian from the Taos pueblo. We pulled him out of the car, and he lay on the side of the road with his head in my lap.

"Do you know how to die?" I asked.

He said, "Yes."

"Are you ready to die?"

He said, "Yes."

I said, "I'll hold you until it's over." I looked up to the horizon. I saw the two death angels. They were leading a long line of people toward the sunset. They waved.

I didn't see them again until they came to take my father "home" two years later. Since then, I've been grieving when I hear of death. My life's work has become at least partially about teaching people to grieve.

JOURNEY THROUGH THE KEENING SPACE

★

Leslie Lynne

I was very young, only twenty-two, full of hope and inspiration, with a desire to give love and support to birthing mothers. After months of attending childbirth preparation classes with our local lay midwives, I finally had earned their trust enough for them to invite me to attend births as a labor support person.

On the physical level, hours of studying anatomy and the physiology of labor had prepared me for the intensity involved in giving birth. My own spiritual practice gave me direct and palpable contact with our loving Source daily. This had prepared me for the sacred nature of childbirth. My divine communion had also made visible to me the radiant souls of my fellow humans.

With great excitement, I attended my first few births. Witnessing birth turned out to be tedious, exciting, a direct plug-in to heaven, and the most earthy, bloody, and messy event I had ever encountered. I loved it. One of the things I noticed most at each birth was the degree to which the souls of all present who were awaiting the arrival of the child were more tangibly visible than at any other time. I saw their souls' radiant light ripple out to interweave and form a fabric of human relationship. This fabric is especially strong in a birthing room because the gate between life and death is open, wide and clear, in preparation for a newborn soul's arrival.

The portal that occurs at birth between the worlds once gave me an experience of mystical travel that led me to the healer's path I walk today.

I was on call for a birth one evening. The hour grew late and I felt it would be best to catch up on sleep in case I was called out in the wee hours of the morning, which is when most babies arrive. With great care I stretched the phone cord in order to put the phone just outside my bedroom door.

Deep in sleep, I began to dream. The wind whistled through dark and keening space. I was in motion: walking, gliding. The walls of my dream world had opened and I was being embraced by the core of life itself. I felt my way through the darkness alone, calling on faith and an immense feeling of love to guide me. My destination was completely unknown to me.

I arrived in the home of the woman whose birth I was committed to attend that night. I walked to the left corner of the room facing the bed and knew I should stand and witness. The midwife, Becca, was on the bed with the birthing mother. The father held a newborn. I felt great distress and the presence of death in the room. Becca was working to help the mother, Rose, deliver her placenta in an effort to stop the hemorrhaging of her lifeblood.

With great concern I called out over and over again to Becca. "It's time to act. Go now! Give up and take her to the hospital. Her life is at an ebb. She's hanging by a thread!" Frustration and tension mounted as I helplessly witnessed the midwife working over the mother. I could feel Rose's life force begin to leave the room. Then, I heard the baby cry. From a place of instinct and intuition deep within me, I turned and began to lead the way out of the room. The moment I did this, the death energy withdrew.

The whistling wind ceased. Light returned. There was a swirl of clear, loving light spiraling into my heart and solar plexus from the four corners of the room. Becca got off the bed. A phone call was made. I knew mother and child were now out of danger. I walked back through the tunnel and into my own bed.

Two days later I had a conversation with Becca. She told me the tale of the birth. I had missed being called to go with her because my phone cord had been accidentally pulled off the phone the night before when I stretched the cord out. I had missed the "earth-based" call to attend this particular birth. Thank God. The heavenly call is what allowed me to give the most help.

Becca told me that Rose had indeed hemorrhaged severely after giving birth. She related to me how she had frantically worked to stop the blood flow and how she had been fraught with indecision about a trip to the hospital. Like any midwife, she had wanted to honor the mother's desire to give birth at home; and in this case the signs were that Rose's condition was improving. The hemorrhage kept appearing to stop but would then begin again even worse than before. She explained to me that Rose was losing vital signs and approaching shock when Becca happened to feel called to look into the left-hand corner of the room. The very same corner where I had stood watching during my dream.

She perceived strong loving energy in that corner and felt deeply guided to take her client to the hospital immediately. Upon arriving at the hospital, the mother needed two transfusions. She had indeed been close to death.

Shaking, I sat down in my chair. How could this be possible? Where had I gone? What part of me had traveled? What road had I taken? And how had I returned?

I had no doubt in my mind that the full force of my soul had been present in the room that night. Although I had always believed in God and spirituality and had in fact had other psychic experiences, I now lived with the concrete reality that there is a spirit world. I knew, because of the road I had traveled in my dream and the guidance I had received at my destination, that there is, in the spirit world, a loving and helpful presence that seeks our good. My journey that night also taught me that the best way to teach and reach others is to walk in the light of truth yourself.

I thank God that I was allowed to help a new family be born without tragedy. And I thank the Divine Mother for the overwhelming sense of her loving presence that accompanies me still on my path through life.

TIME TRAVEL

★

Julie Isaac

Plagued by a series of mysterious illnesses during my early twenties, I had been examined by doctor after doctor, but none succeeded in discovering the cause. So I searched for answers beyond the boundaries of medical science, exploring holistic health, vegetarianism, and spirituality. Of my experiences during that period, what remains most vivid are the past lives I recalled.

On March 4, 1980, I had my first session with Nancy, a past life regression counselor. She began by taking me through several preliminary drills. The first drill established the difference between memory and imagination. She instructed me to remember a situation as it actually happened, then add imagined events to the memory while being aware of how these two types of visualization differed. I found that the scene from memory flowed easily, brimming with texture, color, and sound, while the imagined scene felt forced and flat, lacking memory's depth of detail.

The second drill, intended to help me identify my own body, reenacted an argument my best friend and I had in high school. Nancy asked me to imagine the event from my friend's point of view. Attempting this, my mind rebelled; I simultaneously looked out of my friend's eyes and saw her face. Only a return to my own point of view brought clarity and relief.

Nancy then took me through a drill that focused on opening up my senses of sight, sound, taste, touch, and smell, followed by an exercise on trusting my first impressions.

After spending an hour in preparatory work, we were ready to begin the past life regression.

Of all the feelings surrounding my mysterious illnesses, frustration stood out most prominently. Nancy asked me a series of questions about this frustration that established it was small, dark gray in color, made a banging sound, was centered in my stomach, and made me feel absolutely helpless. She then asked me to start traveling backward in time, to situations in my life when I had felt a similar frustration.

I thought of my trip to London the previous year, when I was hospitalized for a week and my tour group flew home without me. Then I remembered the helplessness and hurt I felt at my parents' divorce, when I was five.

Nancy urged me even further back, to a time when I was in the womb feeling a wordless frustration at the difficulties of my birth. "Is this a new feeling," she asked, "or have you felt it before?"

I hesitated, searching my feelings, my memory, my being. Digging deep. "It feels familiar."

"Then go back beyond this lifetime," she said, "to another time you felt this frustration." My first impression was of being in a covered wagon. I wondered if there were others behind me, perhaps a wagon train, yet I was aware of only one—mine.

But my point of view kept shifting. As in the earlier drill, I seemed to be looking through my eyes and seeing myself at the same time. And what I saw was a dark-haired young man, rugged and frail. "This doesn't feel real," I told Nancy.

"Then let's move on to another memory," she said. I saw myself next in a European court during the Middle Ages. Again, I was a man.

"This doesn't feel real either." Beginning to feel frustrated in the here and now, I tried to relax and trust the process.

Nancy encouraged me to keep going, and I found myself back on the prairie in that same tattered wagon. This time I knew that I was absolutely alone. My name was Robert. I looked down and saw the muscles in my forearms straining as I reined in the horses, my skin a dark golden hue from growing up in the sun. My clothes were rough and ragged, my boots scratched and covered with dust. I'd been on this journey a long time. Wherever I looked, my eyes met only rocks and sagebrush.

"What's dark gray?" Nancy asked, referring to her notes.

"There are mountains on the horizon," I said. "And the sky. It's dusk."

"What's banging?"

I concentrated for a moment. "That's the sound of the wagon as it rolls over the rocks, then hits the ground."

"What's small?" she asked.

"I am," I said, "in the midst of this immense valley." A deep awareness of my insignificance sent waves of terror and awe flowing through my body.

"What's the feeling in your stomach?"

"Hunger." As I said the word, I knew the truth behind it. Starvation. I wouldn't live through this journey. His journey. My journey.

"Why are you doing this?" she asked.

"To prove that I don't need anyone's help, that I can survive on my own." I could feel Robert's pride, also his frustration and fear. "To test my strength." Robert's pride began to crumble and turn to anger. "Why did I let others bully me into this? If I weren't so pigheaded I wouldn't be here now." But his anger was no longer able to shield him from the truth. "Why do I have to die to prove my value as a man?"

Nancy asked me to change the negatives in this situation into positives. Finding it difficult to switch instantly between feeling Robert's pain and putting a positive spin on his experience, I took several deep breaths in an attempt to return to the present. I told Nancy that I wouldn't have made the journey alone but would have organized a wagon train. And that I would have recognized that being a man means more than strength or independence.

Intellectually, of course, I knew that I couldn't impose 1980s values on an 1880s man, and that, as a woman, I was not the best judge of what it means to be a man in any era. But this experience was about healing not history, about learning from the past in order to change the present, so I put aside my judgments and trusted the process.

In Robert's life I found a key to my own. A hundred years on, I still lived in a self-imposed isolation, always trying to prove my emotional strength, my inner worth, and, above all, my self-sufficiency.

While Robert's journey revealed no specific clues as to the

cause of my medical problems, I took the lessons I learned from him as a prescription for health. From Robert I learned the importance of community, how to let people in and my feelings out. How to ask for help. Eventually, my physical problems subsided, and I believe that Robert played a vital role in my healing.

Over the years I have seen proven in my life, and the lives of others, the mind's infinite desire and capacity to bring us back to wholeness. Consciousness uses whatever avenue we open to it—whether that is meditation, visualization, prayer, positive thinking, psychology, or past life regression—to show us the ways we block the flow of our own energy and how to free it again.

Robert may or may not have lived, but he does live in me. And I will forever be grateful for the lessons he taught me.

SPIRITUAL AWAKENINGS

Mark Gonzaga

"You have five to eight years before the virus . . . develops."
I was numb. "Develops?" And everything went white.
My story begins in 1993, the year I was diagnosed HIV positive. Time suddenly impeded the necessity for my life to be fulfilled, at the age of thirty-two. In a flash, the mundane chores and simple fears of life had no meaning as I immediately whisked off to travel the globe.

I was brought up Catholic, attending a traditional Catholic school, uniform and all. You know, God, Jesus, Mary, and the Holy Spirit. Well, I don't suspect the sisters of St. Barnabas were preparing me for the epiphany I was about to experience as my life continued to gain momentum. Next stop, Hong Kong.

I signed up at the hotel for an excursion tour to the shrine of Buddha. As a seasoned, expert traveler, I'd discovered that these inclusive tours are stupendous deals. Transportation, sightseeing, culture, and all the food you can eat, all for one extremely reasonable rate.

I arrived at the shrine of Buddha nonplussed. I had not realized the imagelike shrine was about as huge as the Statue of Liberty. Picture the Statute of Liberty seated with her legs crossed. From broad daylight into darkness upon entering, the spiritual transition I experienced was ecliptic.

"Oumm . . ." drifted through an air of infinitesimal peace and reverence whilst the indigenous worshipers bowed their heads, their hands clasped together, toward a focal point: a glass box.

I joined the procession, although not quite as somnambulistic, toward a five-foot-by-five-foot glass box encased in metal bars. Inside was a picture of Siddhartha Gautama, Buddha, alongside a string of jade green beads and a minuscule bone fragment among ashes.

I looked around, dazed by what I was seeing. The unity I experienced, ensconced within the shrine, could not compare to anything reminiscent of my Catholic church and school or Western life.

"This is it," I said to myself as I knelt on both knees and grasped onto the bars. "You obviously must have existed. You are a powerful spirit. Christ, Buddha, or one and the same, whoever you are, listen: I'm HIV positive. I am not ready to leave this earth plane. I promise you, if you see to it that I don't die of this virus, I'll devote my life to helping humanity."

At that moment my body was lifted. Inside, I was lifted. And I heard a voice: "You will be the one." I was dumbfounded.

I returned to Los Angeles and remained in my home, for days on end. Life was beautiful yet chaotic, people rushing, rushing to and fro. Is this what life is all about? How am I supposed to keep this promise I've made?

I questioned my sanity. Something happened to me. Well, whatever spoke to me was going to tell me what to do. I was certain about that. I had never truly woken up to life as through this spiritual awakening. I prayed at night and asked for guidance. The following year, an opportunity was proposed to take a journey to Israel. I accepted.

Let's cut to the chase. I arrived in Jerusalem. Destination: the Church of Ascension, through hordes of tourists and devotees.

My senses were intoxicated by frankincense as I grew nearer to the most holy of places. In the center of the expansive dome above was a spotlight of the sun shining down through a porthole onto the Hershey's Kiss–topped shrine housing the cave intended to be the final resting place of Jesus Christ. Candles glistening inside emanated a glowing penumbra. Golden chalices of frankincense hung above the slab of rock, adorned by flowers, where the body of Jesus Christ had risen.

This moment was mine, mutually respected by the incessant influx of hungering people. A quiet madness prevailed here, unlike the disciplined reverence at the shrine of Buddha.

I knelt among the flowers, resting my forearms respectfully upon the edge of the slab of rock. I brought my hands together in prayer to commune with Jesus Christ as my eyes were fixed on His image gracing a fittingly elaborate picture frame of cascading silver.

"All right, here I am." I reiterated to Jesus Christ of my awakening in Hong Kong, and I asked for guidance. "Where do I go next?"

As if tapped by the hand of divinity, I felt a tingle settle within me. I bowed my head with a blessing and thanked this revered spirit for touching my life. "I love you."

I parted the shrine, and a woman approached me waving her hands frantically above my head while speaking in tongues. "I'm not crazy, I'm not crazy," she spat out. "I've never seen anything like it. When you knelt where Christ's body had risen from, a blue light surrounded your body. I've never seen anything like it. It was the veil of Mary," she proclaimed fervently. "I heard a voice," the stranger announced. "I've never heard a voice before. The voice said you were chosen."

This was the connection I had journeyed to Jerusalem looking for. This time I had not been the one to hear a voice, I am relieved to admit.

I returned to Los Angeles once again, and I asked for further guidance. Where would I be led to next on my personal journey? I waited for the universe to deliver the answer.

The following year, yet another opportunity for travel transpired. It is said there is no such thing as a coincidence. I'm not quite certain of that, but I had always wanted to travel to Easter Island. Off I went to the navel of the earth, our planet's most remote island in the center of the Pacific Ocean.

Said and done. I had a personal experience visiting the multitude of tall stone Moai statues with austere faces sprinkled throughout Easter Island, steeped in mystery and folklore but nothing more. *C'est la vie*.

Back home in Los Angeles, I sat at my table to write and something unusual occurred. In a trance state, I arose from the table, walked to the full-length window, and knelt with my hands together in prayer, looking up to the sky, waiting. My hands parted, my palms facing outward. I remained in this position for quite a while.

This ritual continued every day for a couple of weeks, dissipating to every other day, to once a week, and now occasionally. And I wondered.

Two days after my first trance I was visited by Bonnie, a woman with a sixth sense who is now a friend. I handed Bonnie the pebbles from near the Moai statues and asked her if she could feel anything.

"Ohhh, these are not of this earth," exclaimed Bonnie. "I mean, they are, but . . . I see blue light." I showed Bonnie a postcard of the Moai statues as she confided to me, "These statues were elevated with blue light. The people who built them were in a trance, controlled by forces not of this earth."

My personal journey of extraordinary experiences continues, leading me to believe that all things unfold as they are meant to. I suppose it was simply my time to be spiritually awoken; and my time, not as simply, happens to be this lifetime. In keeping with my promise to devote my life to helping humanity, I volunteer my time where I can to improve the human condition.

No, I don't know what it means to have been "chosen" or to be "the one." Time will provide the answers. This story could be the answer or the beginning of an answer. As I write these words, I realize that very possibly I could have been chosen to write this story and I am the one to enlighten you of my enlightenment: that it's a big universe out there, and who is to say that one of you reading this has not already been chosen to enlighten all of us?

DREAMTIME DHARMA

★

Jeremiah Abrams

In May 1974 I had a dream that was to change my life. In the dream, I found myself back in my Pennsylvania hometown, a small mountain town, headed east on one of the roads that led out of town, South Street. I am walking, and I meet a person with a donkey, a most unusual, easygoing animal, on whose forehead are carved, in relief, a crescent moon bisected by an inset jeweled star that I recognize as Venus. The person tells me that I should continue going east to the Far East, to the Himalayas, and there I will find what I need.

I awoke from this dream with the image of the moon and star clearly in my mind and didn't think much more about it. Later that week I was talking to a good friend, Rick, and the subject of trekking in the Himalayas came up. He said he had always wanted to do that and I perked up. "Yes, I might be interested in going, too," I said, thinking about the dream message. From that day on it was a foregone conclusion that Rick and I would go to Nepal. We began researching and making plans, and before long it was September and we were on a Pan Am flight headed to Delhi and then on to Kathmandu for six weeks.

Now I had always loved to hike. Mountains were very holy places for me. I traveled in order to experience the mountains in various parts of the United States and Europe, to get to the rarefied atmosphere above the tree line, where it feels like you are in the spirit, in the land of the gods. The Himalayas were the epitome for me, the goal of every mountain lover, and here we were. Headed for the ultimate trekking experience! I was very glad I listened to the dream, though I never shared it with Rick.

There were hardships ahead, however. Delhi was hot and crowded, and Royal Nepal Airlines, our connecting airline, had never heard of us or any of the other 130 people stranded that day at Delhi airport. So Pan Am put us up in the upscale Ashoka Hotel for a week while they sorted out our passage. Rick was Type A about the whole thing, and he went to the airport every day to advance our cause. He had just finished his training as a doctor and was not comfortable with being out of control. India is, in my experience, a much better place to be if you can give up control and open to its rhythms. Finally, Rick pushed hard enough to organize the entire group of dispossessed passengers and chartered an Air India 727 to take us to our destination.

During that stay in Delhi, we rescued an American woman, Lorna, who was in the same predicament and was grateful to have company. She had been to India and Nepal many times before and in turn became our savior down the road. When we arrived in Kathmandu, Lorna took us out to meet her friend Paul at the far western rim of the mountain bowl that makes the Kathmandu Valley. She was on a journey to be with her Tibetan master, and we were appreciative of the connections. We stayed there for several days, getting our bearings and finding our way around the cities of the valley.

In 1974 there were very few amenities; Western ways were just beginning to infiltrate the capital of this tiny Himalayan kingdom. Rick and I got our trekking permits put in order and decided to do a loop to the northern Nepalese border with Tibet, hoping we could cross into Tibet. The border was just barely opened there, depending on political and weather conditions. If not, we would be able to return from the Langtang Valley via an 18,000-foot pass, drop down to 14,000 feet to a Hindu pilgrimage lake called Gosainkund, trek south to the major east–west route, and then choose to go either toward Mt. Everest in the east or back to Kathmandu.

Two days out on the trail with our packs, we were feeling the effects of hiking in a foreign country. It was very hot, there were not many provisions for water or food along the way, and we were not yet in top condition. We had started at about 2,500 feet, the elevation of the Kathmandu Valley, in tropical climate with banana trees, and were working our way up toward the temperate rhododendron forests (between 5,000 and 7,000 feet), then on up to tundra at 8,000 feet, and the tree line at about 11,000 feet.

That second day two Sherpa brothers in their twenties or thirties passed us going in the opposite direction. They asked where we were headed. When we told them, they said we needed them and they would be willing to turn around and guide us. We looked at each other and smiled, and within an hour we had negotiated with Binbatu and Singalama to carry our weight and guide us. They seemed sent to us like angels to make our journey tolerable, and I was greatly relieved.

Both men walked barefoot on the mountain tracks, even with heavy packs. Binbatu was younger but more experienced with expeditions; Singalama was strong and silent. After two more days we came to a yak cheese factory at about 9,000 feet. We were low on protein, so we bought yak butter from the father-son proprietors. The passes were subject to snow, and the Tibetan frontier turned out to be closed because the road was not passable due to slides. Coming over the pass we met an Indian expedition who had lost two men in avalanche. We proceeded cautiously to Gosainkund. Just on our arrival at the site, I began to feel weak. I thought it might be a touch of altitude sickness, and I lay down in the stone hut by the lake while the others prepared the camp.

Trying to acclimate and sleep it off, I fell into a deep feverish state. I awoke that night in a sweat, my temples pounding, and aching all over. Since Rick was a physician, we had every medicine known to mankind with us, and he began doctoring me. Binbatu and Singalama looked apprehensive, like something was terribly wrong, and they slept sitting up with their machetes drawn. I slept.

One day, two days, three days of delirium. On the fourth day Rick said no medication was working, my fever was off the charts, and Binbatu was convinced evil spirits possessed me. I felt like I was dying. I could hardly speak, and when I did I was speaking in tongues. I had dream delusions of being the great snake that was carved on the giant stone rounds outside our door at the ritual site and I was molting my skin. I was in trouble. Since we were a week away from any hospital and had no way to contact anyone, the only solution would be to move on.

On the fifth day Rick roused me and said I would have to hike out, there was a village at 11,000 feet, a full day's trek away. I would have to walk in this delirious state or face deterioration from the altitude, dehydration, and probable food poisoning from rancid yak butter. There was no choice. I walked that day on air. I'm not sure how I managed; it was perhaps the longest day of my life. Only the reptile mind in me was functioning, instinctually surviving.

Distances are distorted in the Himalayas; you can see laid out ahead of you in the landscape where you will be in two or three days. Finally, after what seemed like weeks, we arrived at the village, a highland outpost where yak herders gathered their cattle in precipitous corrals and young Tibetan monks trained in a *gompa,* a mountain retreat monastery. Binbatu found an elder Tibetan householder who agreed to take us in. It was a large extended family, very present and spiritual. They laid me by their hearth. Binbatu bought their fattest chicken, chopped its head and plucked it, and got some protein in me. The walking had actually gotten my juices flowing, and I was only semicomatose now. The change in altitude helped; I was on the other side of the black pit I had been in. The Tibetan's three-year-old grandson attached himself to me and sat in my lap. I slept by the fire that night and awoke the next day, back from the dead.

The Tibetan family was very kind to me. In the morning they said prayers and gave me special foods. We walked out in the village to the corrals, where there was a festival blessing the herd. I carried the young boy in my arms, and everyone stared at me like I was an apparition. We took photos with the whole community.

That night I walked out under the stars, grateful just to be feeling a little stronger. I looked up at the clear heavens and was awestruck: the bright crescent moon was bisected by the twinkling evening star, Venus. Was this the sign I needed? I took it as such, that I was going to be okay, that these were auspicious surroundings, and that something had moved and changed inside of me, deep inside. We left the next day, hiking twenty to twenty-five miles a day.

Back in Kathmandu, I met an itinerant Indian swami hand

reader in a coffeehouse who read my palms and told me I would
meet three women in the next month, each of whom would look
into my eyes and want to be with me and I would respond, but
that I would go west with the third one. This all came to pass.
But the startling connection on my return to the United States
was with the Tibetans. It turned out that our damsel-in-distress,
Lorna from L.A., was deeply connected to His Holiness the
Karmapa, spiritual leader of the Kagyu lineage of Tibetan Buddhism. With the hospitality of that kindly Tibetan mountain
family in mind, I became involved in helping bring the Buddhist
dharma to the West, receiving the teachings and blessings of the
lineage holders, and coming to an entirely new understanding of
my life purpose.

10,000 BUDDHAS

★

Frances Heussenstamm, Ph.D.

October 1979

On my way into mainland China with mostly Stanford University Medical School faculty and wives, immediately after the country opened to Westerners for the first time since 1949. We began with three days in Hong Kong. I shared a room with child psychiatrist Betsy Walloch, from Tulsa, who was as passionate about jade sculpture as I was about embroidered textiles. We went shopping from dawn to dusk for two and a half days and finally paused to unpack it all in our hotel room. Whew!

Mindlessly flipping through a travel guidebook, I stopped suddenly when the words "Temple of the 10,000 Buddhas" lit up in the middle of a page on the left side. I said to Betsy, "I have to go there," and picked up my handbag to leave. She said, "Of course."

We took a train from the island beneath the harbor to mainland Kowloon and debarked at Sha Tin, a little village, muddy from recent rain. I could see a spire in the distance above the trees and said, with some assurance, "That must be it." We slogged our way to the foot of the 10,000 steps we had to climb. Well, it seemed like 10,000 steps at the time.

Chuffing and panting, we emerged, at last, on the edge of a large paved terrace directly in front of an ancient temple. In the center of the courtyard was an enormous classic Chinese red-pillar gate, beneath which sat a gigantic statue of a woman adorned in a pink kimono with figures upon it. I approached the statue with Western curiosity, nothing more. From a distance she looked like the Dragon Lady from the "Terry and the Pirates" comic strip of my childhood.

However, when I looked up into that face—because she towered above me—I began to weep with recognition and familiarity. My conscious mind did not know who she was; nevertheless, in some deep place inside me I knew her. Betsy had the grace to leave me alone with my uncontrollable tears. At last, I regained my composure and walked into the temple.

As I entered, a gong sounded. I knew exactly what to do, although I had never been taught. I went straight to the altar, fell on my knees, and touched my forehead to the ground three times. Before me were four golden images of the Buddha, and ringing the walls were the 10,000 small versions of the Enlightened One. A flood of memories of Buddhist practice filled my consciousness. At that moment I thought, I'm tuned in to the spiritual energy of this place, and how wonderful it is to be able to pick up these vibrations, like a radio that tunes to a particular station. And there was more to come.

I tried to explain to Betsy what had happened, and she was as loving and supportive as I was shaken. The next day we entered China via railroad through old Canton. I was fine until, time after time, I began to weep when we visited old Buddhist ruins, converted temples, monuments, and memorial stele. Soon I hid in the shadows, covering my face with tissues to hide the runny nose and red eyes. Everyone thought I had a cold. But I knew Buddhism from some ancient place in my unconscious.

The minute I returned to my private psychology practice in Santa Monica, three members from the Nichiren Shoshu Buddhist sect appeared and began therapy with me. They taught me their version of Buddhism. Their arrival was a first and immediate confirmation of the significance of my memorable and moving experiences at the temples in China. Another confirmation was a dream of a past life of mine as a novitiate nun in a Buddhist monastery-convent in ancient Japan.

Since that trip, made over twenty years ago, I have explored past lives in therapy and made a study of all the world's major religions. These have vastly enriched my work. Going to the Temple of the 10,000 Buddhas was a personal turning point, and I can gratefully say that it has made a profound and lasting impact on my life.

AT THE SIGN OF THREE
CROSSES

★

Peggy J. Cain

My half sister Cecilia had lived in Louisville, Kentucky, for several years and loved it very much. The last time I went to visit her there she asked me to hold one of her necklaces and see what I could pick up from it. She knew I had a talent for reading vibrations from objects that belonged to people; I often did it as a game. Sometimes it worked and sometimes it did not. I never took it seriously, until that day.

I took hold of my sister's small necklace and thought about it for a few minutes. I did not like what I picked up, and I hesitated in telling her because it was upsetting. My father died when I was a very small child, and my mother remarried and had three more children. Cecilia was the oldest of those three, and we had always been very close and had much in common. The thought of anything tragic happening to our family was worrisome. I quickly put the necklace down, saying, "Now, you know that what I am going to tell you is not a sure thing, it is just sort of a game."

Cecilia was very close to her father, and what I had picked up was about him and two others. She said, "Oh, go ahead and tell me."

I answered, "I saw three crosses lined up near each other. One had snow around it, meaning it was wintertime."

"Well, what does it mean? Tell me," she demanded.

"I feel the crosses mean deaths," I told her. It had frightened me, because I immediately thought of our mother.

"So, who do you think it may be who will die?" she asked.

"I don't know, but I have a strong feeling one of them may be your father," I answered.

She looked at me strangely and said, "Oh."

Within six months her father died. He soon became very ill from cancer and did not last long. Cecilia took it very hard. I thought of the three crosses. My stepfather's death bothered me more because I was still worried that one of the crosses I'd seen might be my mother's. I am very close to my mother.

Time passed. Six to seven months later, one Saturday morning in July 1997, I received a phone call from a friend of Cecilia's in Louisville. The night before my sister had gone to the emergency room at the hospital; she was very ill. Even as I was quickly making arrangements to be with her there, another phone call came that she had died suddenly from a heart attack. None of the family had even known she was sick that week. She was only forty-four.

I was in shock and quickly called my mother. Of course, she already knew. I packed my luggage and prepared to leave early the following morning. Ironically, instead of going to Louisville, I was now going home to Texas. I decided to drive. It was a ten-hour trip, but I needed that time to think.

On the way I had plenty of time to sort out my head. While driving down that long highway, I had a strong sense my sister was in the car with me. Her presence grew strong and stronger. I began to talk out loud to her. I cried most of the way; I needed to cry. I said out loud, "Okay, Cecilia, if you are with me, then prove it. Tell me something I have forgotten that would make me know you are here right now." My mind was already full of specific thoughts and memories of her life.

All of a sudden, like a lightbulb switching on in a dark closet, the memory of the necklace and the three crosses came to mind. Her death was one of the three crosses! My sister was telling me to remember that day, which no one except the two of us knew about. Then I knew it was she.

Cecilia stayed in that car with me all the way to Texas. She seemed at peace. She was no longer in pain, as she had been the many hours before her death. It seemed as if she kept telling me not to be sad; she was okay. Then she told me something very clearly. When her body arrived at the funeral home in Texas, she wanted me personally to fix her hair and makeup for the funeral.

Finally, I got home to my mother's. Several people were there.

My mother and my aunt had made arrangements that day at the funeral home, and now it was just a waiting game. But the body arrived from the airport late, so the funeral had to be put off another day. Waiting was not easy; everything was ready but the body.

I went to the funeral home with my makeup bag. The funeral director led me down a long hall to a back room. One of my aunts came with me for support. I didn't want Cecilia to look like a clown; I knew she needed her makeup to be soft and natural. As I entered the room I saw the back of her head. My sister lay on a cold stainless steel table. Her hair was very blond, and it looked as if it had been washed. She had been dressed in a beautiful yellow two-piece outfit. I stopped and looked at her for a minute. She looked as though she was sleeping and might wake up at any moment.

Then I put makeup on her. She wore it light, nothing heavy. I had all the right colors. My sister looked like she was finally at peace. After putting on her makeup, I brushed her hair and fixed it the way she wore it. It did not take long. When she was ready, I took off the silver cross I always wore and put it around her neck. I also put a red rose in her hand. "Okay, Cecilia," I said. "It's show time." I said good-bye to her, and we left the room.

I stayed at my mother's after the funeral to help her with papers and chores that had to be done. She was doing much better than I'd expected she would. We spent a lot of time talking about my sister. We both needed to do that. Two days later, at sundown, I was sitting on the sofa across the room from where my mother sat in her chair. We were talking, and I noticed a strong sensation of a presence. I knew who it was—my sister. I sensed her near my mother. I told my mother that I felt Cecilia there with us. She said, "Yes, I know she is. I feel her, too." It was like an old scene, my sister standing beside my mother's chair as she had so many times.

In an instant, I saw my sister very clearly in her yellow two-piece outfit, and she looked wonderful. She was holding up my silver cross necklace to show me she knew I had put it on her.

The look on my face must have been dramatic, because my mother stopped talking and yelled at me, "What is it? What do you see?" Then Cecilia faded as quickly as she had appeared. We had often talked in a casual way about death, and had agreed that whoever went first would let the living one know that there was life after physical death. She had now done this for me. I told my mother what happened and began to cry out of a mixture of sadness and joy.

In the months to come, the third cross was often in my mind. I wondered whom it might represent. I remembered that one of the three crosses I had seen had snow around it—like wintertime. Then one day in January, a year and a half after my sister died, my mother called and told me that Cecilia's ex-husband, Pete, had died. As I thought about it all, it dawned on me that there had been almost exactly eighteen months between each death—the three crosses I saw so close together.

Oddly enough, I have finally learned that when I dream of crosses, or see crosses in a meditation, it means death is coming. It has taken me a long time to accept this sign. For example, I recently saw many crosses, far more than I could count. They were everywhere. I thought it strange and wondered about it. Then I let it go. A few days later there was an enormous earthquake in Turkey, where many thousands of people died. I had known something was to take place, but I had no idea what, to whom, or where it would happen. There was nothing I could do about it.

I always wear a small cross around my neck. I have for years. I have many different kinds. The cross to me has a spiritual meaning—the death of Christ. Perhaps that is why I have been given this particular sign, I don't know. I pray for Cecilia that her soul has found more peace in death than she did in life. But, although I miss her, I am not sad.

THE EAGLE'S GIFT

Josie RavenWing

During the time I lived in Arizona, I spent countless hours wandering out in nature, through the multicolored dunes of the Painted Desert and the mesas of Dinetah (Navajo land). As I discovered a wealth of wonders and places of power, I began to invite groups of people from around the world to weeklong retreats during which I would take them to these power places, do ceremonies, and bathe in the subtle energies of the high desert country.

Although I do not live in Arizona at this time, one of my greatest delights has been to travel there each year to continue offering these Desert Visions retreats. During each retreat participants experience healing, visions, miraculous moments of revelation and omens, and a deep appreciation of the power of Mother Earth.

The most recent Desert Visions had been the best so far, the group being very harmonious and eager to explore the unknown terrain not only of the desert and canyons but of the Spirit as well. Toward the end of the week, one crystalline night, I was by the fireside with a Dineh (Navajo) woman who has assisted me in these retreats for many years, listening to her story. She is the granddaughter of a medicine woman who is slowly preparing to leave this world, a fact that deeply saddens my friend. At the moment she was recounting a series of events that had occurred several years earlier—a tumultuous and sometimes frightening period that was a full-fledged shamanic journey of her spirit.

At the end of her fascinating tale, she turned to me, her dark eyes glowing in the firelight, and stated that because of all that she'd gone through during that time, she was now "owed two eagles." She walked away into the night while I remained by the fire, trying to digest this statement and discern what it might mean. Finding no answers at the time, I gazed into the star-studded skies, pondered the mysteries of the spirit, and eventually wandered off to the comfort of my tent.

Several days after Desert Visions had ended, I began slowly driving homeward, stopping here and there to enjoy some of the magnificent parks of the Southwest that I'd not visited in the past. One of these places was Arches National Park, a vast playground of ancient giants who had formed numerous massive rock arches in the course of their antics. It was a hot, clear summer day, and the sun squeezed glittering beads of sweat from my body as I hiked up the steep trail that led to Delicate Arch. Finally, after wondering how many more hours it would take, I came around the corner of a steep mountain and there it was!

Delicate Arch stands at the far edge of a huge natural stone amphitheater. Just past the arch the cliff drops straight down hundreds of feet, and snowcapped mountains whisper their secrets across in the distance. Not being a person who is really thrilled with heights myself, I nonetheless conquered my fears and wound my way carefully around the edge of the amphitheater, past the multitudes of camera-slung tourists of all nationalities, and arrived at the center of Delicate Arch.

I stood there for some time, absorbing the evident power of this place, then sat off to one side of the arch to contemplate the sheer and dramatic beauty of the view. My heart and spirit filled, and I wanted nothing more than to stand and sing out my praise of this little corner of Creation. However, there were so many people there that I couldn't quite get up the nerve to do so.

Moments later, a raven came out of nowhere and flew so close past me that I could hear the rustle of its feathers in the wind. It proceeded to call out to me and tell me in no uncertain terms that I should go right ahead and sing one of the many sacred songs that I knew from the Native traditions.

How could I deny my namesake?

I arose and walked again into the center of the arch. I filled my lungs and then began to sing from my heart, my belly, my womb, my spirit. My voice echoed throughout the surrounding hills and canyons, and my joy in being alive and present in this magnificent place exploded out of me in a river of sound. All the experiences during Desert Visions were there too—the faces of the participants glowing after their sweat lodge ceremony, eyes filled with mystery after their vision quests, the coyote songs in the night; all this and more had filled me to overflowing and now it poured out of me as a celebration of the Spirit.

After I finished singing the song four times through—four being a number of balance and harmony—I moved from the center of Delicate Arch to the side, noticing peripherally that the many tourists had become totally silent and still during my song. I took my bottle of drinking water, poured some on the side of the arch as an offering, and spoke a quiet prayer that there might always be water for all people, creatures, and plants.

Within no more than thirty seconds of pouring the water, from what had recently been clear blue skies suddenly came tiny drops of cool rain! This light and refreshing rain continued to fall on me as I hiked back down the mountain. As soon as I arrived at my car it stopped, and I said thank you again for the blessing and the way it had made my walk so pleasant.

Shortly thereafter I was on the highway heading homeward once again. The first brushstrokes of sunset were painting the rocks and hills on either side of the road in warm red tones, and I basked in the colors and my love of this land as I drove along.

Suddenly my attention was dragged from the hills to the side of the road, where I caught a fleeting glimpse of something fluttering. Part of me knew immediately what I'd seen, and another part could not believe it. I pulled quickly to the shoulder of the highway and began backing carefully toward the point of the sighting. When I thought I'd arrived, I opened the door of my car and, heart pounding wildly, approached what was on the other side of the car.

There it lay, its feathers fluttering in the late afternoon breezes. It was a young bald eagle, and one that had recently finished its final flight. I immediately knew what had happened—saw the vision clearly in my mind. It had been hunting, and as it dove across the highway intent on its prey, it miscalculated, struck the edge of a passing semi, and fell to the earth as its last breath passed from its body. It was young and not yet experienced in the ways of man-made traffic, and so there it lay, power brought down from the heavens like the rain of only an hour earlier, now resting at my feet.

I immediately made a tobacco offering and blessing ceremony for the eagle's spirit journey. Then, knowing I simply could not leave its body lying there to possibly be mauled by passing vehicles or ravaged by the vultures that would inevitably arrive, I gathered it up in my arms. For the moment, it was a child that the heavens had given me to care for.

Once I had the eagle bundled safely in the cooler I kept in the backseat of the car, I began to drive and pray about what I should do with it. The eagle's spirit was a tangible presence behind me, and I sang to it and praised its hunting spirit and its strength, alternately weeping and entranced with its power.

It swiftly became clear to me what must be done. I saw the dark eyes glowing by the fire, and heard her voice telling me she was owed two eagles.

And so I gave the granddaughter of a medicine woman the eagle as a gift to her, to her grandmother for all she'd passed on to her, and to the Dineh, the People. The first of the two eagles had been delivered through me, through the blessings of rain and of songs drifting through the opening of Delicate Arch, through the advice of the raven, through the will of Spirit.

IV

Prophecy and Omens

THE FORTUNE-TELLING BIRDS OF HONG KONG

★

Arielle Ford

Janet and I arrived at the Hong Kong airport on December 30 after a whirlwind week in New Delhi. While collecting our suitcases we ran into our friend David, who had just had a big fight with his fiancée, Pam. His fiancée was so angry that she caught a flight back to the United States, while David decided to cool off in Hong Kong.

Janet, David, and I decided that the easiest way to see Hong Kong would be to take a guided bus tour. Our tour guide was a funny young woman named Ling, who told us all the usual historical data while giving us a bit of the local flavor. Ling said that if we really wanted to have a magical experience, we should go to the night market and have our fortunes told by the birds.

The next night, New Year's Eve, Janet chose to go to bed early while David and I decided to be adventurous and see if we could find the "fortune-telling birds." All we knew was that the birds were somewhere in the night market. Ling had told us which subway to take, but not much else. So there we were at 9:00 P.M. on New Year's Eve, boarding a Hong Kong subway with thousands of Chinese people, in search of the unknown.

At our stop we got back into the streets and began asking directions to the night market. It was just a few blocks away. When we arrived we were on a very long street brimming with stalls filled with all kinds of food, live fish just waiting to be someone's dinner, T-shirts, and unidentifiable objects for sale. We began to stop and ask people if they could tell us where the "fortune-telling birds" were. Those that spoke English and understood us laughed and pointed down the street.

We walked for nearly a half hour, continuously asking for directions and always getting the same laugh with a pointed finger down the street. Soon, at the end of the night market street, we found many tables set up with palm readers. We asked one of them where the birds were and she said, "Birds no good, have palm read." We didn't buy it. We wanted birds. So we asked someone else, who told us just to keep walking and we would find them around the corner. Finally we came to a sidewalk with a few "bird readers."

We sat down and carefully watched what was going on. In front of us was a little old Chinese man with a very long, white beard. He had four cages, each containing a small bird that looked similar to a finch. On the ground in front of him were about a hundred long envelopes, and each envelope had a number written on the outside of it with several Chinese characters next to it.

A customer would ask the Chinese man a question. The man would then ask the question to one of the birds. He would let the bird out of his cage, and the bird would hop around and use its beak to push through all the envelopes. Then the bird would pull one of the envelopes from the pile with its beak and give it to the man. The man would give the bird a treat and put it back into its cage. The Chinese man would take a sheet of paper out of the selected envelope and tell the customer his fortune. Then he would put the sheet of paper back in the envelope and shove the envelope back into the pile.

The Chinese man then asked a different bird the same question. The second bird came out, hopped around, and miraculously chose the exact same envelope again, confirming for the man and his customer that the first fortune selected had been the correct one.

Although David and I could not understand a word that was being said, we fully knew what was happening because we could see the numbers on the outside of the envelopes and figured it out. After watching the process for forty-five minutes, David and I were very anxious to have our fortunes told. By now a large crowd had gathered, and we had been speaking with a college girl from Singapore. She was fluent in many languages and asked us if we would like for her to act as our interpreter. We quickly agreed!

I was feeling a little nervous, so David went first. He asked the Chinese man what he should do about his relationship with his fiancée, since it seemed to be failing miserably. Our interpreter told the Chinese man what David wanted to know. The Chinese man asked the birds, and here is what the birds said: "Even though this is a very difficult relationship at times, you were meant to be together. You are to marry this woman and have children with her."

Now it was my turn. I asked if I was ever going to get married, since I was already past forty. The answer from the birds was a resounding yes, I would have many opportunities and be married within four years.

We didn't have to wait very long to discover the outcome of the fortunes. When David arrived home, he and Pam decided to get married. Pam got pregnant on their wedding night, and they now have a beautiful baby girl. Seven months after returning from Hong Kong I met my soul mate, and we married one year later.

So the fortune-telling birds of Hong Kong were right! It's just too bad that we will have to travel so far to ask them another question.

THANK YOU, SAI BABA

James F. Twyman

When I arrived at Logan Airport in Boston, I knew that something amazing was about to happen. How could I have known how protected I was, that even my own stubbornness could not keep me from the grace of God? For two days, every sign said to cancel the trip to India, as if something terrible was going to happen if I followed through on my plans. I wasn't listening . . . I didn't want to listen. Thank God I did in the end.

I was scheduled to do a peace concert in New Delhi and to focus a worldwide prayer vigil to heal the terrible rift between India and Pakistan, a dispute that had resulted in both countries showing their power by detonating several atomic bombs. The whole world was on edge, wondering if the insanity would escalate. It was the perfect time, at least from my perspective, to focus on prayer. In the past, in places like Iraq, Northern Ireland, Bosnia, Kosovo, the Middle East, and Serbia, I would do similar events where I would perform the "Peace Concert." Everything was in place, and I was ready to depart for another amazing adventure.

But then everything shifted. A day before I was to leave I received a message from the organization that was sponsoring the concert saying they had to cancel. They were receiving pressure from the Indian government not to help me at all. Other things happened as well that seemed to say: *"Don't go."* But I wasn't listening, in fact that's the kind of thing that motivates me. I'll show them all, I remember thinking. I'm going to India even if I have to sing in the streets.

Then two friends from Toronto called, and I told them what was happening. Their response didn't surprise me. "Pray to Sai

Baba," one of them said. "Ask him to show you what you need to do." I knew that they were very devoted to the Indian saint, and though I had never felt particularly drawn to him, I had heard many stories about his miracles. Why not? I thought. It certainly couldn't hurt. I took a small photograph of Sai Baba into my van and sat there for a moment meditating with it. "Help me, if you can," I said to him. "As far as I'm concerned, I'm going on this journey. If I'm not meant to go then you need to let me know." That was it. I went back into the house and finished making preparations for the trip.

When I arrived at Logan the next day, I got into the American Airlines queue and waited my turn. I was no more than three people away from the front of the line when I heard one of the reservation attendants express dismay at an apparent computer problem. "The whole system has gone down," she said. "It's a worldwide systems failure, and there's nothing we can do." I went to the counter to see what was happening. Just as she had said, the entire American Airlines computer system had crashed, and no one was going anywhere.

"Sir, since you don't have any luggage to check, you can just go straight to the gate and get on board. Explain the problem and they will take care of you." I didn't have a ticket for the first leg of my journey, the flight to New York, but I had to be on that plane, one way or another. If I missed the flight to New York, then I would definitely miss the flight to London, and if that happened then the trip was done. The flights from London to New Delhi were packed for the next week, so it was imperative that I not get behind.

Moments later the gate attendant made an announcement: "I'm sorry, ladies and gentlemen, but this flight to JFK Airport has been canceled. The next available flight will not leave until tomorrow evening." Panic.

"What do I do now?" I screamed inside my head. Maybe another airline. "Yes . . . that's it. I'll get another flight to New York, then I won't miss the flight to London, then everything will be fine." It seemed like a plausible, logical solution. That was when the hammer came down.

I blacked out. But then again, I didn't lose consciousness at all. It was as if I had switched to a different reality, one where I was in India walking down a dimly lit back street somewhere I didn't recognize. It was perfectly real, and I didn't even question the shift. One moment I was in Boston, and the next moment I was in India, and it didn't seem at all strange.

Suddenly someone grabbed me and pulled me behind a building. Then there were two men, not Indians but men in Western clothes. They dragged me behind the building and pulled out knives. Then I felt the pain, the terrible stabbing pain of metal being jabbed into my body. It was as if it was really happening, but then, right before I was ready to scream, everything shifted again.

I was on the subway in Boston heading downtown. It was as if I had been sleepwalking and woke up in a strange place, not at all aware of how I got there. I looked around and wondered what was happening. How did I get here? It was the most confused I have ever been in my life. As soon as the train stopped, I got off and got back on the train that would take me back to the airport. I didn't have my carry-on luggage, and my eyeglasses also had mysteriously disappeared. A half hour had passed, time that I could not explain. Another half hour went by until I arrived back at Logan. The airport was nearly deserted by then. It was midnight, and I wasn't going anywhere.

I finally had to admit defeat. I had done everything possible, but everything had been blocked, as if the universe was determined to keep me on the ground and in the United States. After the vision, I understood why. I would have been killed if I went to India, for whatever reason. The fact that the men who dragged me into the alley were from the West meant that it was more than a random act . . . or at least it would have been. The angels weren't going to let me go, and they had to ground an entire airline to stop me.

When a friend picked me up at the airport and drove me home, I was dazed, still not sure what had happened. I tried to tell my friend, but the words came out confused and disjointed. And yet there was a deep feeling of being safe, protected from whatever harm would have come to me if I actually had got on that flight. Everything seemed to be in perfect order.

The next morning I was at my office and decided to open a few letters. There was one particular envelope that caught my attention. It was a bright color and was larger than the rest. I opened the envelope and took out the stiff piece of paper. It was a drawing—of Sai Baba. The letter was from a man who said he was inspired to draw it for me; he didn't know why. But I did.

Thank you, Sai Baba.

CONVERSATIONS
WITH A BIRD

★

Jill Lublin

Something deep inside of me was urging me to go out into the world—a longing, a calling. I had a thriving business, a beautiful home, an adored cat, good friends, and a relationship with a man whom I loved dearly. Yet the need was so profound, I couldn't ignore it. It was always with me—when I went to sleep, when I woke up, and throughout the day—and it kept poking me in the ribs, reminding me: "There is something more to life, something I need to do or be." I had everything, yet felt unhappy. My life seemed rich on the surface, but inside I was lonely and isolated.

For years I had wanted to interview mystics, healers, and shamans for a book and had never acted on the impulse. When February 1994 arrived, I could no longer ignore it. I put my house up for sale, sold my car, folded my business, gave away my beloved cat, and followed my heart to South America. I had no itinerary, no hotels, no dates, only a backpack and a general direction.

When I had been on the road for three months, my house sold at a financial loss, and a permanent home had still not been found for my cat. She was being shuttled from place to place, not quite fitting in anywhere, and it was causing me a great deal of emotional pain. Here I was, on the journey I had dreamed about taking for so long, and I was feeling bad—very bad. After the initial freedom of being without a schedule, boredom and the fear of being still set in. What would I do—nothing? I didn't know how to do that. I missed my friends and family. "What is so important about this trip?" I asked myself. I felt tired, drained, and exhausted. At times I could hardly move. Week after week of this hopelessness drove me to despair so deep I considered suicide.

Some friends were building a spa and healing center on the beautiful Venezuelan coast, about three hours from Caracas. They invited me to stay in their guest cottage, and I accepted. While there, I made a decision truly to give in to the stillness. I read, stared at the ocean, and dove into any feelings that came up. I sat on the beach watching day turn into night, staring intently to identify the exact moment that day became night. I watched, night after night, and could never be sure. Darkness descended, but it was impossible to detect that moment when light turned into darkness. It seemed to reflect my emotional process at the time. I would be feeling fine, and then . . . wham, something would hit me and I felt depressed, sad, lonely, or alone. These feelings had become more intense over the course of two weeks.

One night I left the beach and wandered back to my room to prepare for dinner with my friends. I went to the closet, began looking through my clothes, and suddenly a small bird flew out and landed on the bookshelf across the room. He was a plain bird, dark brown with no special markings. He pressed himself up against the shelf so he wouldn't fall off, raised his wing, and turned to the side so I had a view of his profile.

Still in a state of surprise, I looked deeply into the bird's eye. My body began to vibrate, and then shake. I had been a long-time meditator, but I had never felt anything like this. My rational mind wondered if the bird was hurt, while a trance state was enveloping me, taking me deeper into the experience.

The bird began to change form before my eyes, and I spontaneously started to chant and then sing to him: "Fly with me, I am with you; fly high with me." My back straightened; my arms seemed to rise without effort, stretching out as if to fly. Suddenly, I began to cry. I was sobbing deeply, bawling and wailing. I felt so many past hurts at once—a symphony of pain—and I cried wholeheartedly for close to an hour and a half. Therapy had never been like this!

The bird never moved or made a sound. It sat motionless on the bookshelf, watching me. When my emotional breakdown subsided, a profound sense of happiness filled my body. The bird turned and looked me squarely in the eye. I felt drained and empty, but a cathartic release had taken place.

Earlier that day I had found a large feather as I was walking, and now I offered it to the bird, setting it in front of him on the bookshelf. I thanked him for having come to me and left the room to take a shower.

Afterward, as I was headed downstairs to dinner, I heard an insistent "cheep, cheep, cheep" coming from my room. The bird hadn't spoken before; I decided I had better listen. I went upstairs, entered the room, and saw the bird, now sitting on my bedpost under my reading lamp. He looked directly at me and stopped chirping.

I was relaxed and open. What have I forgotten? I wondered. The words came: "Tell him you love him." As I did that, his small throat wobbled excitedly and he spoke again with his high-pitched cheeps. I was certain that, somehow, he had understood.

I asked the bird to be my guide for the rest of my travels, for him to allow me to fly on his spirit wings through my trip in this world, and to remind me to go lightly and with love on this earth journey. I offered him a sticker with the image of the earth on it, repositioned the feather near him, and went down for dinner.

When I returned a few hours later, the bird had again switched positions and settled on my bed, over to one side. The same inner voice that had prompted me to begin my journey told me to sleep in the other bed. I asked the bird to speak to me while I was asleep if there was anything I needed to know. He remained where he was as I slipped into bed, fell asleep, and entered the dreamtime.

When I awoke in the morning, the bird was gone. The feather was lying down near the end of my bed, and the earth sticker was now on top of my medicine card deck. I've had intense experiences with nature, but never have I had Spirit visit me in such direct form. After this encounter, I faced the long and unknown journey ahead of me with new strength. I no longer felt alone; I knew Spirit was watching over me. My encounter with the plain but magical bird had reassured me that I was not alone. As I packed my few belongings for Costa Rica, the next leg of my sojourn, I took the spirit of my bird connection with me.

Dear little bird, wherever you are in your flight, may you continue to guide me on mine. Let me fly on your wings, that I may soar on your path. May I fly with purpose and presence on this earthly journey. May my own wings grow stronger and freer and more joyfully expressed with each passing day.

THROUGH MY FATHER'S EYES

★

Gail Albert

I first experienced the gifts of compassion, awareness, and love through my father's kind eyes. All I had to do was watch the kind way he opened his heart each and every day. Life filled him with laughter and joy, whether he was feeding an old, stray cat, saying friendly hellos when we would walk to town, or sharing stories of the Old West. He once told me that "anyone who can make a person laugh with a good story has the world by the 'tale.' " His tender approach to life taught me how to find harmony and face any challenges that might come my way.

Shortly after my father's ninetieth birthday, I made plans to travel to Borneo, Bali, and Australia, where I would meet up with my husband. Not long before my departure date, my father took ill with the flu and a fever. Even though the symptoms were minimal, in my heart I knew it was the beginning of my dad's journey beyond space and time. I hoped that his preparation for this divine venture would be a gradual and graceful process.

Daddy and I always had an unexplained bond between us. No matter if they were stories of Tibet, Africa, or even a small town in Iowa, he would sit by the hour as I shared my life experiences. He loved to hear about the people and animals. No matter in how much detail I described the sights, sounds, and spirit of these explorations, he always wanted to know more. He would sit like a wide-eyed child in wonderment. It was as if he were walking side by side with me and feeling the same magic I had.

My loved ones were not happy that I was traveling at such a crucial time, considering Dad's age and illness, so I decided to let him make the decision. When I asked, he looked up from his hospital bed with a slight chuckle and said, "If you don't make this trip, how will I ever hear about Borneo?" He promised he would wait for my return with great anticipation. Nevertheless, my sister Linda was very afraid, and as a result my heart was filled with mixed emotions.

I boarded the plane, still encouraged by the memory of Dad's words to me, yet fearful of leaving my sister in pain. Going down the narrow rivers of Borneo, seeing sights and surprises around every bend, I was constantly aware of Dad's presence, knowing how his eyes would sparkle and treasure every precious wonder. After leaving Borneo, I flew down to Bali, where an extraordinary event occurred.

I awoke one morning feeling very ill. Something unsettling gave me a cold shudder, and a moment of fear came over me. Instead of taking my morning time for meditation and prayer, I called for my Balinese guide. My mind was racing with thoughts of Daddy and my sister's loneliness. For once in my father's life, I did not think he would be able to keep his promise. I asked the guide to take me to a Buddhist temple. There, through tears and prayer, I stayed and meditated for several hours.

Suddenly, I noticed an old man carrying a huge python around his neck. As I watched him and saw the connection he had with the snake, a feeling of peace came over me. He let me hold the snake, and I became consumed by the harmony and music shared by all creatures. It was at that moment I knew my father was still alive, although his passage was soon to begin. I needed to return to California as soon as possible.

That very same day, a transformation occurred in my father's hospital room. He had taken a turn for the worse, and my sister was sitting quietly by his bedside. She told me later that all at once Dad sat up with outstretched arms and called my name. He kept asking Linda if she could see me and kept asking me to come closer to his bed. He asked my sister why he wasn't able to touch me. In her bewilderment, Linda tried to explain that I was still in Bali and would be coming home soon, yet he insisted that I was there in the room, just out of reach.

On my arrival in the United States, I immediately went to my father. My dad's first words were of how glad he was to know I was home and how very sick he was, and then, "Now, tell me about Borneo." I hugged him for a long time and cried tears of joy. My sister and I decided to take Dad out of the hospital and bring him home for his new cycle of life. We had three beautiful weeks with him, shared by his two granddaughters, my daughter, Gena, and my sister's daughter, Julie. We laughed and told stories—even Dad told a few. We talked openly of his passage and shared how Dad's courage brought inspiration and hope to us all. It was a true gift of time to express our love and admiration for one another.

Dad's passing from this life to the next was harmonious, gentle, and very peaceful. It took only about fifteen minutes when Dad decided to leave his old, worn, but not yet rusty body behind. We stepped aside so he could make his new connection. He knew we were there, although his flight to freedom was for him alone.

I cannot explain what happened on that special day in Bali, or what happened at the same time in that hospital room half a world away. Nor do I wish to try. Through my father's kind eyes, I have the acceptance that he is ever present, awaiting another story. Well, Dad, there you have it.

DEEPAK'S MUSHROOM OMELETTE

★

Arielle Ford

Christmas, 1998, my husband, Brian, and I went on an extensive holiday to Egypt and India with a large group that included Deepak Chopra and his wife, Rita. The first ten days in Egypt were spent cruising down the Nile visiting ancient temples and pyramids; it was beautiful, magical, and everything we had hoped it would be. While we were there, the United States began bombing Iraq because Saddam Hussein was refusing to cooperate. Since we didn't have ongoing access to American newspapers or television, we didn't hear much about it until our last few days in Cairo, when we were finally able to watch CNN. It all seemed very scary to me, especially since we were getting ready to leave for India. What if we got caught in the middle of fighting?

Our flight plans called for us to fly Egypt Air to Jidda, Saudi Arabia, and then to change airlines. From Jidda, we were scheduled to fly Saudi Arabian airlines to New Delhi. For some reason this was the most direct route to India. Our last night in Egypt concluded with a fabulous feast at our hotel overlooking the pyramids and a show of Egyptian dancing and music.

We arrived at the Cairo airport around 10:00 P.M. and almost immediately encountered problems. Because of security issues, our tour guide was not allowed to go to the ticket counter with us. The man at the Egypt Air counter spoke very little English. We handed him our tickets, and he disappeared for about fifteen minutes. When he returned, he told us that we could not board the aircraft, pointed to an area of chairs, and told us to go sit down.

The airport was very crowded and very busy, and I was quite nervous because our flight was scheduled to leave in ninety min-

utes and we didn't know what was going on. In the middle of
this chaos Deepak said to me, "I'm hungry and I would like to
eat a mushroom omelette." I told Deepak he would have to wait,
that we didn't have time to find a restaurant, and, besides, he
had just eaten a large dinner.

Twenty minutes later another Egypt Air person arrived and
told us that the reason we couldn't board the aircraft was because they had just faxed Jidda to see if our Saudi Air flight was
still scheduled to fly to New Delhi. Since we didn't have visas to
be in Saudi Arabia, they could not let us board the flight to Jidda
until they were certain we would actually be boarding the flight
to New Delhi. Because the United States was bombing Iraq, no
one was certain which flights were still operating.

We now had thirty minutes until our flight was scheduled to
depart. Someone had just reminded us that at midnight the Muslim holy month of Ramadan would begin. During Ramadan,
Muslims fast during the day, and no food would be available.
Deepak also reminded the three of us that he was still hungry
and wanted a mushroom omelette. We told him that as soon as
we arrived at his mother's house in New Delhi we would be sure
to get him a mushroom omelette. With ten minutes before takeoff, they finally let us board the plane, although no one bothered
to tell us whether or not our flight to India would be operating.

The three-hour flight to Jidda was mostly uneventful. When
we landed, the sun was just rising over the desert. The airport
was filled with Muslims in their white robes. We could hear
chanting as the morning call to prayer filled the air. In the middle of the airport there were rugs on the floor so that the men
could kneel and pray on one side while the women kneeled and
prayed behind some screens on the other side of the terminal.

Once inside the airport we found a transit desk. A very sweet
and friendly young man who knew a few words of English offered to help us find our way. We were clearly the only Americans in the airport. Once we located our luggage, a guard with a
scary-looking gun motioned to us to follow him. We were taken
to a small room. Once we were there, the guard took our tickets
and passports and left us alone for about one hour.

Deepak again reminded us that he still wanted a mushroom

omelette. He was in a great mood and fascinated by all of the activity in the airport. I was terrified. There were guards with guns everywhere, and none of them looked happy to see us. No one spoke English, and we had no idea when or if we would be going to India.

Another guard came, returned our tickets and passports to us, and placed us on a bus. We had no idea where we were headed. The bus took us to another terminal, where another guard with a gun took us to another small room and again took away our tickets and passports. Some time later this guard returned our tickets and passports and walked us through a huge underground walkway that opened into yet another terminal. At this point someone told us that our plane would be taking off for India, but that it was delayed five hours.

Finally on our own, without any guards glaring at us, we realized we were now stuck in the Jidda international terminal. The place was filled to capacity. A giant board with electronic letters listed all the various flight information. Deepak spotted a neon sign that featured a coffee cup. Assuming it was a restaurant, he again told us he wanted a mushroom omelette, and we followed him in the direction of the sign. When we got there we discovered that it was indeed a restaurant, but it was closed.

It was now the first day of Ramadan; everyone was fasting, and no food was being served. No mushroom omelette for Deepak. I was too scared to eat anyway. The one really bright note to the day was that this terminal had a beautiful gold jewelry store and it was open. It had some of the most beautiful gold jewelry I had ever seen and at excellent prices. Rita and I spent most of our time buying jewelry while Deepak and Brian had a great time people watching. Finally the big electronic board announced that our flight was boarding. We stood in a very long line waiting to clear security. It wasn't as simple as it was in the United States—all of us were taken into small closets and given a thorough search. Once they determined that we were harmless, we finally boarded our Saudi Air flight to India.

It was now late afternoon. We were tired, hungry, and very relieved to finally be on our way. We buckled our seat belts, and the plane took off. Once we were airborne the flight attendant changed out of the traditional Muslim dress that covered her entire face and body into a typical Western flight attendant's uniform. She took her serving cart over to Deepak and said, "Sir, may I serve you a mushroom omelette?"

You can imagine our shock, as she said those words. Deepak had been asking for a mushroom omelette for sixteen hours, and now he was finally getting it. We all ate our mushroom omelettes and then fell asleep for the rest of the flight.

The next day I asked Deepak, "Did the mushroom omelette appear because you desired it or did you desire the mushroom omelette because you somehow knew that it was on the way?" His answer was "Both!" He then went on to explain to me the Heisenberg uncertainty principle, which is the quantum physics explanation for what happened.

My explanation? If you want something bad enough it will happen!

MATCHMAKERS IN
HEAVEN

Lora Vivas

The term *soul mate* was new to me in my early adult years. It seems to have just popped onto the scene of my consciousness somewhere during graduate school. None of the long-term relationships I had experienced came near to what I imagined a soul mate would provide. During graduate school I took a short trip with a good friend to San Francisco. We did all the tourist things and a lot of the local things, and that was that. I wasn't looking for my soul mate. I had a great time but planned to return to Austin, Texas, and continue my life there.

The first night back in Austin, I had a vivid dream in which I felt my body spin upward into what seemed to be another dimension. Upon arrival in the "other place," I found myself talking to my grandmother Abuelita, who had passed on some three years earlier. The message I received from her was to return to San Francisco, something I had no intention of doing any time soon, and certainly for nothing more than a visit. The dream left me with a racing heart and unsure mind. I became compelled to get myself back to that magical city by the bay.

I managed to land an internship at the Levi Strauss world headquarters in San Francisco, where I worked for six months. I planned to fill the summer months that followed with any fun, active job and then return again to Austin. After a series of shot-in-the-dark phone calls looking for the ideal summer job, I was finally referred to an inner-city YMCA. When I went in for the interview, I had long forgotten my dream with Abuelita. I was merely interested in having fun and paying my rent for a few more months in this beautiful city.

As weeks passed, I noticed that while working with my boss (the man who had interviewed me) there was a certain electricity between us. At first I let it go since he wasn't what I had defined as "my type." Soon, however, I couldn't deny the chemistry. Within weeks we were dating and sure that our union was cosmically created. We chose to marry on New Year's Eve in a private ceremony.

The night we married my husband told me that when I walked into his office for the job interview, a voice in his head told him clearly, "This is the girl you are going to marry." We had both received messages that guided us to our destiny together. We joked that there must be matchmakers in heaven.

Now we believe that those matchmakers were the children we brought into the world a few years later. Nearly nine years and two children later, our paths have led us to a very spiritual place. Looking back, though, I realize that our paths also began from a very spiritual place. We have continued to have experiences that confirm our belief that listening to the voice within leads one to the perfect place every time.

REMEMBER TODAY

Roger Clevenger

When I was a child, my father's father and I were best friends; we did everything together. Grandpa was and always will be my soul mate. Unfortunately I lost him to cancer in 1985. At the time I was in the military and had to race home to see him before he passed away. I made it from Lawton, Oklahoma, to his hospital bed in Springfield, Illinois, in what I am sure was a record time. What my family didn't know was that when they called my first sergeant to ask the Army to send me home, I had already requested my leave to go be with my grandfather.

I don't know why, but I just knew to get packed on the morning of June 25, 1985; I was going home to him. The family knew that Grandpa was sick, but he had never told anyone until that day just how bad it was. I made it to the hospital an hour before visiting hours were over. He sent my grandmother home. He told her that I was there and she should get some rest; she needed to get a good night's sleep.

It was extremely upsetting to see his coal black hair turned gray and falling out. Grandpa had been having chemotherapy, but it wasn't working. You could tell it was too late. My grandfather made me sneak to the cafeteria and get him a large cup of coffee. Then I wedged a chair under his doorknob and we drank coffee, smoked cigarettes (those were what killed him), and got to talk one last time. He told me he wished he could go home to die.

As the evening wore on, the nurse came by and berated us for the smokes. Gramps asked her, "What is it going to do, kill me?" He broke out laughing and coughing. Slowly he got to be less and less coherent. He kept telling me to "remember today, not tomorrow or yesterday. One day or the other doesn't matter."

Finally, at about 11:00 P.M., he and the nurses kicked me out and told me to go home. I told him I loved him and would be back in the morning.

He replied, "Earlier than you think."

My parents' house was an hour away from the hospital, and I was just too tired to drive. The night was warm and gentle, and I decided just to sit out in the car and sleep there.

I hadn't dozed off for long when I awoke sobbing. I knew things weren't right. It was about 12:30 on June 26. I went back into the hospital to check on my grandfather, and the nurse said that she had just that minute called my grandmother to tell her he had passed away in his sleep at 12:05 or thereabouts. In my mind, all I kept hearing was, "Remember today, not tomorrow or yesterday." The nurses, doctor, and I argued about the time. After a yelling match, the doc looked at me and said, "One day or the other doesn't matter." When he said that I gave up.

Every year after that on June 25, I wake up to Grandpa's memory and his words, "Remember today, not tomorrow or yesterday." In 1990 my wife, Kim, and I were due to have a child in June. On the twenty-fifth I got up to his words screaming in my ears. I started laughing and crying. I know Kim thought I was nuts. Zachary Mitchell was born that day.

Five years later I took my wife and our three children graveyard hopping, to show them where all my father's family was. We have seven generations of tombstones in a two-county area. I hadn't been out to my grandfather's tombstone for years. There never really was a need, since we talk in my dreams all the time. When I need him most, I can always feel him with me. The last stone I went to see was my grandparents'. Grandma had passed on in 1987. Kim held the kids back for a few moments when we got to the cemetery. She knows that Grandpa and I talk all the time.

As I sat at his stone and talked, Zach, who was five then, couldn't stand it any longer and came running to me and hugged me. He said, "Why are you crying, Daddy?"

I told him I felt bad because I hadn't been out to Grandpa's tombstone in so long.

Zach's exact reply was, "Remember today, not tomorrow or yesterday."

V

Divine Intervention: Healing, Prayer, and Meditation

SIDLING HILL

Nancy E. Myer

I was traveling east on the Pennsylvania Turnpike from my home in Greensburg, Pennsylvania. It was a glorious day. The Laurel Mountains were dressed for the occasion in wild oranges, yellows, and vivid magentas. The sun shone down, highlighting the wide variety of colors. I had come over the crest and was driving down a long, slow grade. In front of me was a large semi with a tarp-covered load. He sounded like he was having a little trouble with his gears.

The tag says Ohio, he's probably not used to our mountains, I thought to myself. Sidling Hill rest stop is just ahead; I'm going to take a break to ease my complaining shoulders. The semi's turn signal flicked on too.

I dropped well back as I realized that the driver was going too fast for the sharp curve in the exit. Just as I thought it, the truck groaned and started to tip. I hit the brakes, watching in horror as the truck turned over in slow motion. The load must have shifted. I glanced around; I was the only person there. I could not see the exit coming from the other direction; I hoped someone was on that ramp.

The truck hit the ground with a sickening crash and flipped the cab over, like a kid playing crack the whip. My car and I rattled around from the two impacts.

I drove onto the berm and turned on my blinkers. Then I ran over to the truck. The load—gravel—was spilling out around the tarp. No wonder it had shifted so slowly.

As I ran up, I found myself beside the mountainous truck. I smelled fuel; I glanced under the cab and saw a slow leak. This is not good, I thought.

I walked around the nose of the cab. I could see the driver

through the cracked windshield. He appeared to be in a lot of pain. Blood was smeared all over the windshield, making it hard for me to tell where he was hurt. The only practical way for me to get up on that truck was to climb up the grille and inch across the side of the cab to the driver's window. One more glance around for help. I'm it; fuel is dripping away.

I reached up, as far as I could, pulling myself up on the grille. It was sturdy enough to hold my weight. I'd been out on a terrain search with some cops and hadn't changed out of my hiking boots. I was glad of it now; they would brace me better than tennis shoes would.

The side of the truck was slippery, but I was able to hang on and get across to the window. I peered down into the trashed cab. Blood and junk were everywhere. Beneath the mess I could see the driver. Oh no. He was absolutely huge.

He stared up at me in surprise. "Lady, you need to get us some help. Me and my partner's hurt bad. I think my leg's broke. I know my arm is. I got to get off of him so he can breathe. He's not making a sound under me."

"There's someone under you?"

"Yessum, my buddy's under me. I weigh, well a lot, and I'm worried he can't breathe. How big are you?"

"Well, I'm five foot nine and a half and I . . . well, I'm not too big, but I'm motivated. Fuel is dripping from one of your tanks."

"Shit, we gotta get out of here."

Looking around for someplace to attach my legs, I realized the big side-view mirror was in the perfect spot. I shoved and kicked it, to see if it was solid enough. I twisted my legs around it and leaned as far down into the cab as I could reach.

He stretched up; our hands just managed to grasp. "Do you have one good leg?"

"I believe I do." He mopped the blood out of his eyes.

"Okay, on the count of three you push and I'll pull. One, two, three . . ." With all the strength we could muster, he barely moved at all. I thought I heard someone calling, just as he started to cry. The pain of his broken limbs must have been excruciating.

I hauled myself back out of the cab, hoping for a large man.

I found a diminutive old lady waving her hankie up at me. "Do you need help? Is anyone hurt?"

"There are two men in the cab. Both of them are badly hurt. Fuel is leaking from one of the tanks. They're awfully big guys, I can't get them out. Please get some help."

"I'll dial nine-one-one at the rest stop; I'll get you lots of help." She bustled over to her car and floored it.

Back down into the cab. "Did we move you enough to help?"

" 'Fraid not, missy. I'm just too heavy for you to lift."

"Is that a sheet next to you?"

"Yeah."

"Hand it to me." Stretching down into the cab again, I grabbed the sheet. I tied it around me, shoulder to waist diagonally. I hoped the knot would hold.

"Grab the end of this sheet with your good hand, hold on to it. When I count to three I'll pull, you push."

"Oooh, damn. Sorry, miss. It hurts a lot when I move."

"That's okay. You just swear, scream, whatever it takes—just push as hard as you can."

I braced my feet carefully against the doorframe. When I was sure my position would hold, I counted, "One, two, three . . . rrrrrrh!" I was hauling for all I was worth, and I could feel a little movement, but not nearly enough.

We rested and went at it again. As I braced, I looked up at the sky and prayed, "God, please get me some help." I leaned into the sheet.

I felt him before I saw him. A great sense of peace descended on me. I knew an angel had arrived. Large arms reached around me and grabbed the sheet. The glowing hands pulled with us, and the injured man started to come out of the cab. I nearly fell off my perch with that pull.

I leaned over to see where the angel was; the driver was bracing with his good leg and his back, partway up to the window. "I can hear him breathing now. But I can't hold this position, can you give another big yank like that one?" I looked at the angel.

He smiled. "Coming right up. Ready?"

"Ready when you are."

"One, two, three . . ."

As his head emerged from the window, the driver grabbed desperately at the doorframe with his one good hand. When he let go of the sheet, he started to fall back in the truck. The angel and I, gripping his good arm, kept on heaving. This guy was really heavy. He came through the window slowly, so large he had to squeeze hard to get through. He looked at us and stopped, his mouth gaping. "Is that an angel you have helping you? Or am I nuts?"

"No, you're not nuts. I asked God to help, and He answered. Let's get you the rest of the way out."

"I need to catch my breath. I'm hurtin' bad."

We both sat there gasping for breath as the angel, keeping me from falling off the truck with one hand, reached to touch the trucker with the other.

As the angel touched him, his head came up; his whole body was surrounded by glowing light. "Lord, I will never doubt you again," he said, looking up at the sky. I knew the angel was giving him strength so we could get him the rest of the way out. In the distance, I thought I heard a siren.

Pulling hard again, we managed to drag him out of the cab. He was huge. We hung on to the side of the truck, our lungs heaving for air. His right arm dangled uselessly. So did his left leg. He was pretty well covered in blood. I could see cuts across his forehead. Luckily, his eyes seemed fine, although the blood kept running in them. We needed to get him to the ground before he passed out.

Using the sheet again, the angel and I lowered him down across the motor to the ground. I called out to him, "Can you crawl away from the truck?"

"I can, but I won't. Can you see a fire extinguisher in that cab somewhere?"

I leaned back into the cab and gasped in shock. Another man, just as big as the first, lay in a mangled heap at the bottom of the cab. He appeared to be unconscious. The fire extinguisher was not visible.

"I can't see it."

"Can you see a shovel wedged behind the driver's seat?"

"Yes." I pulled it out.

"Toss it down here, I'm going to try and shovel some of this gravel on the fuel."

I tried to toss the shovel near him, without hitting him. He grabbed it and waved the shovel at me as he started crawling toward the shifted load and leaking tank.

Back to the task at hand. With no conscious response, it was going to be a lot harder to get this man out. The sickening smell of fuel was getting worse. I could hear shoveling from the driver as he tried to keep a fire from starting.

I was going to have to climb into the cab. There was no other way. I looked at the angel and was startled to see that he now looked like a regular person. A huge man dressed in jeans, plaid shirt, and work boots.

The siren arrived; the car had barely stopped when the trooper hit the deck running, fire extinguisher in hand. He ran around the bottom side of the truck and started spraying away.

The angel lowered me into the cab quickly. I tied the sheet carefully around the unconscious man. I prayed that he didn't have a broken neck, but the risk of fire was too great to wait.

The angel hoisted me back up; together we started hauling on the sheet. The trooper clambered up beside us; he pulled too. Between the three of us, we got the trucker unwedged and starting to move. We had to stop for air. The fuel smell was beginning to make me sick.

The angel placed his hand on my chest and stomach, and the sickness left. We pulled mightily, managing to drag him halfway up the cab.

A brief rest, and back at it again. We had him out!

The trooper and the angel carefully lowered the trucker to the ground, then carried him over to the cruiser. I was too tired to move. The angel, seeing me still up on the truck, jumped up and helped me down. Then he disappeared, as quickly as he had come.

"Dang. I never thought I'd see one of those," the man with the shovel said as he tried to crawl farther away from the truck.

The trooper reached inside his trunk and came up with a blanket. He spread it on the ground, rolled the injured man onto it, and then we pulled him away from the truck together.

Looking around puzzled, the trooper asked, "Where'd the big guy go?"

"That wasn't a guy, that was a really big angel." The first trucker I'd helped out of the wreck sighed. "A really big angel." He passed out from his pain.

The trooper smiled. "I guess he's seeing things."

"Nope, he was telling the truth. I prayed for help, God sent an angel, and then He sent you."

"But he looked so normal. Are you sure?"

"He looked like an angel when he got here; he changed into looking like a man, just as you arrived. I guess he didn't want to waste time with explanations. If you think about it, have you ever seen a man that big before?"

The trooper braced himself against his car. It had finally hit him . . . he had seen an angel. Shaking his head in confusion, he reached into the cruiser for his radio. "Where are those fire trucks? We've got a semi about to blow out here!"

I plunked down on the ground beside the truckers, too tired to move a single muscle. I hoped the truck didn't blow up. I didn't have the energy to move.

I saw a flicker of light under the truck.

The trooper grabbed his fire extinguisher and ran at the flicker, spraying. The angel stood up, laughing, as he brushed foam off himself. The trooper stared at the huge angel as it unfurled its wings and disappeared again.

He sprayed down the small flames that were starting up, shaking his head in disbelief. This was not in the police manual. I wondered if he'd ever dare tell people.

A fleet of ambulances and fire trucks flew up the ramps, coming from both directions.

Dog tired but feeling wonderful, I dragged myself back to my car. The trooper waved me past the accident, saluting as I passed. I waved happily.

I was used to angels. This was all new to him.

ANGEL WITH A LANTERN

★

Jill H. Lawrence

The year was 1964—long before angels were in vogue. I had just graduated from Northwestern University that June, and three of us who were sorority sisters had planned a mini-reunion in August. Sue and I decided we would fly to New York and visit Judy in Darien, Connecticut, for a remember-when weekend. We were psyched!

Susie was from Milwaukee, and I had grown up in Canton, Ohio. Neither city was even a remote match for New York City, but after four years at Northwestern and becoming extremely comfortable getting around Chicago, I decided I was a "big city girl" and felt undaunted by any metropolitan area. Bring 'em on was my attitude!

So it was without a second thought that I suggested to Susie that we do the tourist thing in New York and go see the Rockettes before going out to Darien. Susie, however, wondered aloud if it was such a good idea to be taking a train out to Darien at such a late hour. I waved away her concern with a flick of my hand. I assured her we'd have no problems. After all, we had conquered Chicago, and New York wasn't going to faze us either. Famous last words.

We flew into New York on the agreed-upon date, checked our luggage in a locker, went to Radio City Music Hall to see the high-kicking legends do their thing, and had a great time. Afterward, we grabbed our bags, hopped on a train, and headed for Darien, where Judy was going to pick us up.

The train ride gave the two of us a great opportunity to re-hash the fun we had just had, and we both agreed seeing the Rockettes had been just the thing to do.

The train came to a halt at our stop, and what happened next is still so clear in my mind it's as if it happened yesterday. We stepped off the train pretty much in tandem. Susie was to my right. I remember the wooden elevated platform that was under our feet. It surprised me that we were above street level and would have to descend some stairs to find Judy and the waiting car.

The train pulled away, and we began to take a few steps. I was struck by the fact that we were utterly in the dark. Not a single light shone as we began to make our way across the plat-. form to the steps that we could barely see.

We assumed Judy was at the bottom of the stairs waiting for us, but we could not see her and she could not see us. We were alone in the dark on the elevated platform—or at least that's what I thought.

We had taken only a half dozen steps when out of nowhere a gang of thugs appeared. Soundlessly, one young man stepped in front of us to stop our forward passage. I turned my head to appraise the situation and saw that one gang member was positioned to Susie's right; when I looked to my left, I saw a swarthy young man naked from the waist up. I will never forget his torso and arms. They were studded with countless pieces of gauze that had been stuck into wounds to stanch bleeding. The coagulated blood held the gauze pieces in at least a dozen locations, giving him a bizarre "decorated" look.

I never fully turned around to see who was behind us, but at least one person was there because I heard him speak something unintelligible.

I had the same experience as others who recount crisis and emergency situations—everything goes into slow motion, and this was no exception. Undoubtedly, all of this happened in a matter of seconds, but it felt like minutes while I assessed the situation. I remember the thought passing through my mind. This is not good. I had yet to get in touch with feelings of fear as I was still mentally taking stock.

I do not remember what our would-be attackers said; I only remember the menacing stances and the desperation of the situation. Just the two of us. In the dark. No one to see us. No one to help.

Then suddenly, out of literally nowhere, a man strode toward us. He came from the open track area across the platform. He struck me as a virtual giant of a man. He was wearing an engineer's outfit complete with hat and was carrying a lantern.

As he strode purposefully across the platform, the gang of thugs parted without a word and without having laid a finger on either one of us. The giant of a man said, "May I escort you young ladies downstairs?"

Susie went first, I followed, and the lantern bearer brought up the rear. We descended the stairs and, sure enough, Judy was in her car at the bottom of the stairs, totally unaware of the near disaster.

Susie jumped in the front seat and I climbed in the back, throwing my suitcase in before getting seated. Although we had thanked the man as we came down the stairs, when I got in the car, I naturally wanted to get his name and address so we could thank him more properly. I turned to talk with him and was startled to discover he was gone. There was simply no sign of him anywhere. Greatly baffled and intensely grateful, we sped off.

Surprisingly, in retrospect, Susie and I didn't talk much about what happened that night. We just sort of dropped it. We knew that we had been incredibly lucky and that something pretty strange had happened that night, but angel intervention never crossed either of our minds. In fact, we really had no way to categorize what had occurred.

Over the years Susie and I exchanged Christmas cards and occasionally visited each other. She still lived in Milwaukee, and I was only ninety minutes away in Evanston, just outside of Chicago. But I don't think we spoke of that night again until I called her to meet me for lunch twenty years later.

For some reason the events of that August night in 1964 never had been fully filed away in the dusty archives of my memories. Every once in a while they would surface into my consciousness. What also were beginning to surface were books on angels that recounted personal angel interventions and life-saving angel stories.

I was struck by the common themes. Angels appeared out of nowhere. The savior angel spoke as few words as possible. The angel pretty much went "poof" and disappeared right after the event. These seemed to be common angel intervention hallmarks.

It dawned on me that those very hallmarks were consistent with my experience, too. Could it have been an angel that saved Susie and me? I wondered. I also wondered what Susie remembered about that night.

We met for lunch in Racine, Wisconsin—halfway between Milwaukee and Evanston. I was so anxious to meet with Susie that I was about to burst. After we placed our order I said, "Susie, do you remember that August night in 1964 when we were going to visit Judy?

"Please tell me every single thing you remember, from beginning to end, without leaving out any details." I held my breath for her answer. I didn't want to plant any ideas in her head, so that was all I said. I wanted her to recount our experience without any more prompting from me.

She remembered our going to see the Rockettes and being on the train going out to Darien. She remembered us getting off the train. She said she had been nervously eyeing a bunch of young toughs who were on the train with us, but my back had been to them and I was completely unaware of their presence.

Once the train pulled away, she said she recalled us being surrounded by those unsavory young men. What happened next was a total blank to her. Nothing. Zero, zip, nada. It was as if a virus had wiped out her hard drive. The screen of her mind was utterly devoid of any memory.

The next thing she remembered was getting in the car with our friend Judy. She looked at me quizzically. "I have no idea how we got from the platform, away from those guys, and safely into the car. No idea whatsoever." I was not a happy camper to hear this. Even when I finally told her what I remembered, she still was blank.

At first I was greatly disappointed, but in a way her memory lapse is even more proof to me that it was an angelic intervention than if she had remembered it exactly as I had. As it turned out, I would experience other verifications.

As my children were born and grew, I naturally did not men-tion the experience I had had. I would never have told them something that could have frightened them. Nonetheless, one of my daughters would corroborate the existence of my angelic engineer.

Lara has been psychic pretty much since she was born. Later she told me what had happened to her when she was four or five years old. She was in bed in her room with the door open to the second-floor landing, where we had a piano and bench. Lara awoke in the middle of the night and looked out to see a man sitting on the piano bench. She remembers him to this day; he was smiling warmly at her and dressed in an engineer's outfit—overalls and a long-sleeved shirt. He was visible to her from the waist up. Despite the fact that he was missing his lower half, and he had appeared in our house in the middle of the night, he did not frighten her in any way. She said she knew he was a kind and loving person. Her childlike acceptance of spirits meant she didn't question who he was or why he was there.

Years later, in the early nineties, I had just moved back to Canton and was having a reading with a Massillon, Ohio, psychic-medium named Judy Greek. I had not repeated my story to her either. Honestly, I don't think I had ever repeated that story to anyone at all. Only Susie.

Nonetheless, Judy told me she was seeing a man who was wearing an engineer's outfit and was leaning against a boxcar. She said he wanted me to know for sure that he would always be there for me.

Well, that was proof positive for me. *Finally.* The pinball machine in my mind lit up as the bells were ringing and the connections were made.

I do know that my life and Susie's life were both saved by a guardian angel back in 1964. Of course, you don't have to believe in angels or be aware of them in order to benefit from their presence. That's the great thing about angels—they *act* like angels and they *do* angelic things without even being asked. In my humble opinion, it's a pretty heavenly arrangement.

POPOCATÉPETL

Donald D. Hartman

It was the winter of 1959. We were a climbing expedition working without ropes on the slopes of Popocatépetl, one of Old Mexico's most lofty and awesome volcanic mountains, which soars almost eighteen thousand feet into the sky overlooking Mexico City, some thirty miles away.

One of the rules of the game is using no ropes with fewer than seven climbers. It takes at least six strong men to hold one if he falls, and we were only three. The point had just been punctuated before our very eyes. Don Osmolak had lost his hold on the mountain only yards from the top and bounced down the face of the glacial ice for somewhere between a thousand and twelve hundred feet.

He made a valiant effort to regain a hold. At his first bounce Osmolak sank his pick deep into the ice, but it only cut a groove and dropped him again. He turned in the air to deliver a second strike. As he slammed shoulder first into the wall of ice, Osmolak drove the pick deep again. This time the ice was firmer. The pick held, but his weight was too much at the speed he had now reached. The pick was ripped from his grip. The third bounce was headfirst. Osmolak was now unconscious.

Joe Garza and I watched helplessly as Osmolak seemed to bounce forever like a rag doll while his pick and only defense dangled in the ice high above.

Finally, his body slid to a grinding stop facedown on the lava stones and volcanic ash that made up the terminal moraine at the end of the glacial ice. Osmolak was only a heartbeat away from a straight drop, which would have been best described as a splatter finish had he gone just inches more.

Neither Garza nor I even considered the possibility that Osmolak could still be alive after the fall he had already made. Still the same, we were working our way down to the body as fast as the dangerously thin air would allow. I retrieved the renegade pick on the way down.

We had about two hundred feet more to go when I saw Osmolak's hand move. He was still alive! But he wouldn't be for long if he moved even a little bit and started to slide. He was beginning to regain consciousness but was not yet aware of his incredibly dangerous situation. We yelled repeatedly for him to remain motionless lest he slide over the edge. There was no response. But fortunately, in spite of his dazed, half-conscious state, he heard, understood, and remained motionless.

When we finally reached Osmolak, we found that the moraine was frozen solid only two or three inches below the surface, thus allowing us to fortify our precarious hold on the mountain with the spikes on our boots while we sought to secure Osmolak's safety as best we could. I drove Osmolak's pick into the frozen ash next to his left shoulder and then mine parallel about a body width apart. We rolled Osmolak face up with the picks placed under each arm like crutches; we hoped he would hang until we could use the third pick to dig a hole in the frozen ground, where we could then place him more or less in a sitting position overlooking the edge of the moraine.

Other than the gash in the top of his head down to the skull and the fact that his body was racked with pain all over, we had no idea about his internal condition. Fortunately, the zero temperature kept the flow of blood to a minimum. This was a major blessing. We were still near seventeen thousand feet high, where one needs every drop of blood to carry oxygen. Even so, if Osmolak were to go into shock, he would die quickly. But Osmolak was tough, Polish stock from Chicago, which served him well. On the negative side, he was also well over six feet tall and weighed at least 220 pounds, sort of a Polish Viking. I, on the other hand, was only five foot ten and 160 pounds. Garza was even smaller. At this altitude it was simple arithmetic. We could not move him, and if we stayed with Osmolak until someone realized that we were overdue, we would probably all die before help arrived.

Even though Garza was a Scotsman who wore a kilt on special occasions, he was born in Mexico and spoke the language without an accent. Therefore, we decided that he should be the one to go for help. I would stay with Osmolak and gamble with the clock.

I gave Osmolak two of our three codeine tablets and held the last one in reserve. I dumped all of our one pack of antiseptic powder into the gash on his head and wrapped it, using up our only roll of gauze.

We watched in silence as Garza disappeared down the mountain. Popocatépetl was in a national park, and there was a ranger station and base camp just below the tree line, at about eleven thousand feet. We could only hope that some climbers would be there with the guts and skills needed.

Popocatépetl is a mountain at the critical height. It can be climbed to the top without oxygen tanks if you are in good shape, don't dawdle at the top, and descend quickly. But one out of three is not good. Granted, in those days we were all as tough as steel nails, but we were forced to dawdle and were not descending. Otherwise, we had chosen our day well for the climb. It had been a balmy zero degrees and sunny all day. But as the sun sank toward the horizon, so did the temperature.

Even while resting, breathing was extremely difficult. We began to shiver. We were out of water and food. Using up any body heat to melt ice for a drink, even a taste, was a serious no-no. I became ever more certain that had I been able to spit, it would have surely frozen in midair and rolled away like a rock.

Osmolak's watch had been flattened at about 4:00 P.M. I tried not to let him catch me looking at mine. We could see for miles, but there was no sign of Garza. I tried not to wonder what else might have gone wrong.

Even though we were so high that it was still bright sunshine where we were, we could see the darkness spilling over the earth below, deeper and deeper, like a strange ethereal tide climbing the mountain face toward us with stealth no lion could match. So it came as no surprise when Osmolak put words to what we had both been thinking. "There is nothing more you can do. Leave me."

We began to analyze how best to play the bad hand we had

been dealt. I gave him what I thought I could spare and still make it. Climbing would generate heat, and each step toward the valley would bring up the surrounding temperature a small fraction. I wrapped his face with my scarf and gave him my gloves. I had already ripped the cardboard backing out of my pack for him to sit on so that his bottom would not be directly against the permafrost. Osmolak folded his arms against his chest inside of my empty pack. This later proved to be critically important for his hands. I then filled the space around him with volcanic ash. Any insulation was better than none.

The good-bye did not come easy. I had no way of knowing if I had taken off too much or if he could make it with what little extra I had to give. But our logic was that both of our chances were better this way, if only marginally so for him.

I descended as fast as I could, racing against hypothermia. It was working. Although our crisis had begun much higher, we later learned that earlier that same season seven men had died near the place where Osmolak was marooned. They were roped. One fell and pulled down a second before the team could react. The remaining five went down like dominoes. Together, they had gone over the edge of the moraine.

I reached the door just as the encroaching tide of darkness swallowed the ranger station. But the moon was full, and the ice and snow above were glistening brightly. It would be possible for help to climb by moonlight.

I found Garza inside, but the news was not good. They had radioed for help. But the only climbing teams with the skills for the job were scattered far and wide in Mexico City. It was near midnight when two large vans sputtered up the dirt road with engines strangling for air. There were ten climbers, one a young doctor just out of medical school. Garza and I gave directions, and seven men started out immediately, leaving the doctor and two more behind as a backup team.

In the wee hours they were back, exhausted and unsuccessful. Storms strike without warning at high altitudes. Clouds first blocked the moon and then leaped over the mountaintop with howling winds and blinding snow. The men had been lucky enough not to be too high already for a successful retreat.

Although Garza and I were adamant that a second team should go as soon as the wind and snow stopped, the veteran climbers saw no need to hurry. It was now twenty degrees below zero up there in a driving wind. It was their collective opinion that Osmolak was surely dead by now. But something in me kept saying they could be wrong. In desperation, without even so much as a lowered head, I instinctively prayed in my mind to God's ear alone, "We are all exhausted. If Osmolak is still alive, we must have more help to save him. Help us!"

Night climbs up a mountain, but dawn descends. As the cold gray light slid down the slopes into the first of the tundra grass, we could see several men moving toward us just above the tree line. They were a team of young Germans who just happened to be in our area. But in my present years I am inclined to believe very little in dumb luck and a lot more in guardian angels working overtime. Or in this case perhaps it was a team of Germans conscripted to do angels' work.

Their leader was a redheaded Aryan named Rudy Thareu, who pointed with pride to the place on his passport where it said, "Occupation: Explorer."

As soon as Rudy learned of our situation, he pulled me aside and said, "My men all first learned to walk in the Alps, but we don't have the right gear for higher up. If you can supply us, we will go for your friend."

Within minutes Rudy, Garza, and I had cajoled and shamed the quitters into action and assembled a much more promising second team, consisting of the Mexican backup climbers, including the doctor, and all the Germans.

Then came the critical question from Rudy. Could Garza and I make the climb again to show the way? We agreed to try. Some of the older veterans rolled their eyes in disbelief. Life at such altitudes is really slow death. We had already overextended our bodies, and a second try would be akin to Russian roulette with more than one bullet in the chamber.

We were over halfway there when my legs began to do strange things totally unrelated to my command. I staggered and fell. Fortunately, we were on a gentle slope. The doctor came over, looked in my eyes, felt my pulse, and announced to the others without fanfare, "He's finished." He then gave me a pill that he said would revive me. I was instructed to wait there and re-join them on the way down.

They were only a few hundred yards above me when the pill kicked in. I suddenly felt like trotting on up there, but wisely I decided to stick with the plan. It wasn't until the next evening when I crashed that I found out he had given me industrial-strength Benzedrine in a dose strong enough to make a dead man get up and dance.

When they reached Osmolak, only his head and the tips of his boots were above an undisturbed new blanket of snow. Again, it was a mixed blessing. The fresh snow, plus the ash, had insulated his body just barely enough from the chill of the bru-tal wind and the twenty-degrees-below-zero night. Osmolak was still alive but incoherent with hypothermia. He, too, was given Benzedrine, then wrapped in a blanket and laced tightly into a light metal rescue stretcher to be lowered by ropes.

Osmolak's pill also kicked in quickly, and when some sem-blance of his rational mind returned, his first emotion was that of sheer terror as he found himself laced tightly in the stretcher dangling on a thin nylon rope while being lowered by men he had never seen before, all of whom were shouting instructions back and forth in German. The last codeine pill had long since run out. Every fiber of his body was in pain except for his lower legs and feet. From the knees down he felt nothing—not a good sign. Osmolak's first conscious thought on top of the terror was that he had died, and this must be some kind of ice hell, and the Nazis were running it all.

By the time they got back down to me, they were past the worst of it and were doing a stumble-along carry of the stretcher. By then Osmolak had made a more accurate appraisal of his sit-uation and was begging them to let him try to walk. The fear of being dropped was too great, and the Benzedrine was giving him false strength. The doctor objected because he knew what was surely hidden in Osmolak's boots, and he was not eager to tell him.

We made a democratic decision as best we could in our newly formed linguistic zoo. Rudy and the other Germans, who had done much of the work and were now prostrate on the ground, used their collective voice between gasps for air to unanimously agree with Osmolak that he should walk if possible now that we were on the easier slopes.

Since Osmolak could not feel his feet, two men walked ahead of him by one step. Osmolak placed his hands on their shoulders and could thereby reasonably control his balance. It worked.

Osmolak spent the next week in the hospital, followed by a couple of more weeks in bed at home, and then onto crutches. Strangely, no bones had been broken. Neither were there any internal injuries of consequence. But the flesh covering the bones was your basic purple. The bandage I had put on his head also covered his ears and pressed them close. So they were saved. By virtue of good gloves and arms folded inside the pack, his hands were saved. Had it not been for the fact that Osmolak was wearing the best of handmade climbing boots, I am sure he would have lost both feet. Even so, his feet were badly frostbitten, and the doctors were indecisive for days. The general structure of his feet was finally saved except for losing one little toe and all of the toenails.

As for Garza and me, we were both lighter and wiser. I had lost twelve pounds during those two days on the mountain, and the ultraviolet rays had cooked the tip of my nose to medium well done. Garza and I were both out of bed in another two days. The Associated Press picked up our story, and it went all over the world. Reporters met Osmolak at the airport when he returned to Chicago. When one of them asked him if he would do it again, he quipped, "Do you know anybody who wants to buy a pair of handmade climbing boots, size sixteen, used only once?"

We all continued for a while as cockeyed celebrities with invitations to fancy parties and movie lots to watch movie stars at work. Eventually people began to ask what we had done lately, to which we replied, "Nothing." So, as quickly as it came, our fame began to melt into the Akashic Records.

Nothing much tangible remains today from the adventure, except for a few yellowed newspaper clippings. My pick and spikes are still in the garage. And I imagine somewhere in

Chicago there is a pair of handmade climbing boots, size sixteen, used only once. But the memory of those days has never dimmed, I suspect because one is more alive when closest to the edge. It is the memories so earned which are the magical souvenirs. And for me the most powerful magical souvenir the mountain could manifest is that secret certainty that one of us would surely be dead had it not been for a team of Germans assigned by God to do angels' work in answer to that simplest of prayers.

The stench of volcanic sulfur is repugnant to most, but to me it whispers the name of that surreal place. It triggers my mind's eye, and I am mentally where I can savor the most precious souvenirs of all; where I can see the curvature of the earth, where I can watch an always spectacular sunrise or sunset, where I can set foot into a perfect ermine crown of snow which no boot has desecrated before, and where the door to God may be as little as one step away under the unbroken drift.

MESSAGE FROM MY MOTHER

★

Kathleen Keith

This was to be a journey of nostalgia, back to Iowa, the state where I was born. I had chosen to travel in October to see the beauty of the leaves of autumn. I walked around the campus of Iowa State University at Ames, visiting buildings where I had attended classes. By noon I had finished. I drove out to the cemetery where both my parents were buried. Their grave sites had flat stones so that mowers could maintain the grounds easily. It was one of those beautiful days of October's bright blue weather, balmy and sunny, with the whole cemetery decorated with gold and red leaves newly fallen from the trees. A truly beautiful place.

I found my parents' grave site easily and meditated for a moment or two. Then I walked up a row. Many of the places were filled since I had last come here. It had been many years. I turned to go. Then I heard my mother's voice, in a commanding tone, "You haven't looked over in the next row, you need to go over there and take a look."

I'll admit to a curiosity hearing her voice, so I went to the next row but found no names of interest. I tried the next row. Nothing there either. I turned around to go back to my car. I heard my mother's voice commanding me to go and check yet another corner of the cemetery.

My final destination that day would be a town in northern Iowa where a high school classmate and her family lived. She was working, so I wanted to have time for a leisurely drive through the Iowa farmlands. I planned to arrive at her house around 5:00 P.M.

It had been pleasant wandering through the cemetery, looking at the names, but I had to keep a schedule. Yet every time
I turned to go back to my car, which was about a hundred feet
away, my mother's voice would tell me to go look in yet another corner of the cemetery. Finally I just marched down
toward my car.

As I reached out my hand to open the car door, my mother's
voice thundered in my head, "*Don't* you *touch* that car door!
You go back up there and look in the far corner. You haven't
looked there yet."

Okay. So back I went. Still I found no names of any real interest.

This was getting pretty silly. I headed for the car again. Once
again my mother's voice commanded me not to touch the car
door. I dropped my hand, then reached for it again. I had spent
forty-five minutes in the cemetery just looking around. It was far
more time than I had intended to spend.

As I got in the car, I heard my mother's voice saying, "No, no,
come back," but I resolutely moved out toward the highway
north out of the city.

The countryside was as beautiful as I remembered. I made
leisurely stops for coffee and also a bathroom call just like clock-
work, every thirty minutes. For some reason, no matter how
hard I pressed down on the accelerator, the car would not go any
faster than thirty-five miles per hour. After an hour the warm fall
day began to dissipate. There was a chill in the air. I even had to
stop and put my coat back on, which I had thrown carelessly in
the backseat. The highway stretched like a gray ribbon straight
north. The farmhouses were very white, and the grass was a
beautiful green.

Now the highway turned from gray to a bright silver. Up
ahead was a dark thundercloud with just a ribbon of light beneath it. It was headed east across my path. Well, I'll just slow
down and let it pass. I really don't want to fight my way through
a rainstorm. Belmond, Iowa, will be my last stop at 3:00 for coffee before I head east, I thought.

The sky even looked different. It was orange-colored. The
grass was brilliant green, and farm buildings were a brilliant
white. If this had been springtime I'd really be worried with the

look of that sky, but this is the autumn time of the year. The cloud looks awfully dark up ahead.

Two miles south of Belmond, the State Police were stopping cars and sending them on a detour east around Belmond. Gosh, no coffee now! "Why the detour?" I asked them.

"There has been a tornado that ripped through the town of Belmond, turned over railway cars, and went right down main street. It hit there at three o'clock."

My blood froze! I had intended to be *in* Belmond at three o'clock at a café drinking coffee. But I was running late, and so I missed the tornado.

In a frenzy, I drove the final thirty minutes into the town where my friend lived. There were trees down everywhere. There was a premature twilight, but lights were on in only a few houses. I arrived at my friend's home and found her wild-eyed with worry for the safety of her children. They were frightened but unharmed.

The next day I got a copy of the newspaper detailing the damage that the out-of-season tornado had done. It showed a picture of downtown Belmond, a café clock which had stopped at 3:05, when the tornado ripped through, and a chain of fifteen railway freight cars overturned on their tracks. There was a report that three tourists who were passing through town had stopped in the café for coffee. They were still in the hospital being treated for cuts by broken glass.

I sent up a prayer of thanks. My mother's voice from the Other Side had delayed me from being in harm's way. In truth she may even have saved my life!

It pays to listen to the messages from the world of Spirit! And beware the tornado-colored landscape and sky!

AMAZING GRACE

★

Lacey Hawk

My memories of childhood include the presence of an angel by the name of Grace. Grace has been with me from as far back as I can remember, and she is with me still.

Four years ago, while living in Colorado, I was spiritually guided to open my heart to making great changes in my life. The first of those changes was to let go of my career and begin a new path of service, which would be hands-on healing. Without hesitation, I joyously accepted this new stretch of my journey and began immediately.

Within a very short span of time, I had developed a reputation for my healing abilities. I received requests and invitations from people in several states. Early on a man phoned me from San Diego; his wife was dying of cancer and he wanted me to fly to California to perform a healing. He felt that her time on earth was very short, as she was in the last stages of the disease. He didn't know where else to turn, so he had turned to alternative healing and found me.

Actually, I must admit that I cannot take full credit for the beautiful gift I have been able to share. The truth is that I do my work with Grace. From the moment I began to heal, I was in training and Grace was my instructor. During a healing session she would guide me. We would connect telepathically, and it felt as though she would step partially into my body, merging her energy with mine. Grace and I became so close during that time that I was always aware of her presence.

I accepted the invitation to go to San Diego, and travel arrangements were made for me. With the urgency in time, the airfares were outrageous. As it turned out, it was much cheaper for me to get to San Diego via San Francisco, although I would need to spend the night in San Francisco and fly the rest of the way the following morning. This arrangement was fine with me, since I had a dear friend in the San Francisco area with whom I would spend the night.

On my initial flight I was worried that I wouldn't make it to San Diego in time to heal the woman. All I could think of was how I wanted so badly to take her in my arms and rid her of the malady that consumed her body. I remember laying my head back and asking her, in my mind, to wait for me. Grace's voice penetrated my senses as she said, "She will pass before you get there, but a healing will take place nonetheless."

Tears came to my eyes, and my throat constricted with emotional pain. My tears were not for the woman whose time had come to cross over but for her husband. He was so desperately in love with his wife, and I knew that the loss for him would feel unbearable.

After my arrival in San Francisco, my friend and I went out to dinner. We gorged ourselves on pasta, and then, just as the dessert was being served, I felt Grace leave me. The left side of my body went numb, and I felt as though a part of myself was missing. My face went pale, and my friend noticed the shift in my energy immediately. She asked what was wrong, and all I could do was shake my head and say, "Grace is gone."

We ate our dessert in silence, as we both felt something was very wrong. My discomfort over the absence of my angel was overwhelming, and I suggested that we go back to my friend's apartment right away.

As we were walking up the stairway, we heard the phone ringing inside. She hurriedly unlocked the door and rushed in to answer it. It was the man in San Diego informing us that his wife had passed on half an hour earlier—the exact time that I felt Grace leave me.

I sat down heavily on the edge of the bed wondering what to do now. I didn't have to contemplate for long. The man wanted me to come to San Diego anyway. He felt he needed me and said he had just had an amazing experience that he would share with me when I got there.

Well, I went, and to this day I am eternally grateful for the miracle that took place the day his wife passed. She was not in the hospital, as her wish was to die in her own bed. She had been upstairs, drifting in and out of consciousness all day. Her pain had been completely gone for several days.

The man left her for a moment and went downstairs to converse with a friend of his who was there. While they were speaking, a bright golden light emanating from his wife's room drew their attention. They looked up, and both men were in awe as they stared at the brilliant light. Then, instantly, it was gone.

The man rushed upstairs and into the room. His wife had passed, and a single tear was visible as it slowly trickled down her blissful face. She had seen the face of an angel, and that angel was Grace.

I knew in the moment he told me his story that although his wife's cancer was not healed, her heart certainly was. Not only had she received a healing that day but the two men did as well. You cannot lay your eyes upon pure love and not have it affect you in some profound way.

MOMENT IN MIDAIR

Judith Wright

It was just us—my husband, Bob, and me—on a beautiful, private Caribbean island in a marvelous villa with no phones, no television, no radio, no e-mail, no fax, and no disturbances. We had nothing to do but spend much-needed time with each other, nature, and God; time to recharge our batteries and prepare ourselves to reenter our lives refreshed and ready to rejoin the workaday world.

Our trip had begun with a high-powered business conference in which we were bombarded with the catastrophic possibilities of Y2K and other natural and man-made threats to our fragile economic and social systems. We had also heard the uplifting story of a unique bank in Bangladesh that provides small loans to women, who use the funds to lift themselves out of extreme states of poverty. Interestingly, the bank's loan repayment rate is slightly more than 98 percent.

But the conference had ended. Now it was time for us to rest and relax. Miles away from our demanding jobs in Chicago, we luxuriated in days of sunning, talking, napping, reading, dreaming, praying, snorkeling, and watching sunsets from our veranda. Over dinner we welcomed the silvery moonrise sparkling across the ocean at the end of each day. And in the evenings we gazed at far-off stars in the cavernous tropical sky.

Our paradise was fleeting, however, as the sand from our precious R & R hourglass slowly began to empty. Abruptly, sadly, our utopian trip had come to an end. It was time to return home.

The morning of our departure was stormy. Cloudy skies and high seas threatened, and the weather seemed to grow more ominous by the hour. Along with another couple from the island, we were taken to a local fishing boat for a short cruise to a nearby island. There we would be transferred to a small six-seater plane and flown to Barbados. From there, we would jet back to Chicago.

The cruise, however, was anything but short—or uneventful. With five- to ten-foot seas crashing into and over both sides of the boat, the trip seemed more like a head-on train collision than the idyllic glide it was supposed to be. At one point the boat tipped so precariously that I slid off my seat into the lap of a fellow passenger, who, by chain reaction, promptly slid onto the heaving deck of the fishing boat.

Quickly disembarking from the docked—but still rocking— fishing boat, we raced to our Barbados-bound plane. The pilot stood next to the aged contraption and affectionately stroked it as we clamored aboard, saying, "She's an ugly pig, but don't worry. She'll get us there." Having only recovered the use of our land legs a few minutes earlier, we barely paid attention to this unsolicited testimonial concerning the sleekness of our aircraft.

Strapped tightly shoulder to shoulder into our small seats, we sat directly behind the pilot, and the other couple sat behind us. The wings outside the window were at eye level, each adorned with propellers that created a monotonous, incessant buzz throughout the flight. About halfway through the one-hour flight, the left engine of the plane suddenly shut down, and we all watched in horror as the propeller turned slower and slower and slower. And then it stopped dead cold.

The pilot turned around to tell us that we could still fly with one engine, but not as far as we had planned. He said that there was no need to worry, all we would need to do was change our destination in order to land safely. My confidence was shattered, however, when he turned back around and I noticed that he was reading a laminated red card entitled "Emergency Instructions." Suddenly it hit me: this was an emergency.

I held Bob's hand and began to pray. I focused on the Maria medallions I was wearing around my neck: mementos of magnificent experiences from pilgrimages I have led, places where I felt the presence of the Divine Mother's love and essence. My mind also raced through the accomplishments of my life: how much of what I set out to do was still incomplete, and how desperately I wanted to continue my work. We sat silently in apprehension—four passengers nervously awaiting a safe landing . . . anywhere.

And then the unthinkable happened. The plane's right engine suddenly went dead. Suddenly, there was absolutely no noise. Our plane was hurtling through the sky without any power whatsoever. The pilot's hands immediately flew in several directions at once, flipping switches up and down with relentless desperation—doggedly trying to restart one of the engines. The four of us, too terrorized to speak to one another, grabbed life vests from under our seats.

Miraculously, the pilot was able to restart the engine after a few frenzied attempts, and the plane began to right itself. Ten minutes later we were on the ground safe and sound, albeit surrounded by fire trucks and other emergency vehicles.

Breathing a sigh of relief, I turned to Bob and told him that I felt as though this were more than just a harrowing experience. "Honey," I said, "God is talking to us. There is a reason this happened, and it isn't just so that we'll have a good story to tell." I told him that I was now able to understand the fragility of life and wanted to cry tears of joy to express my feelings about surviving a terrifying experience.

Bob, however, did not share my feelings. He saw the entire incident as nothing more than a "mechanical thing." The plane didn't blow up or catch fire, he said. He told me that it was wrong to view this as a mystical experience. I told Bob that I thought he was in denial.

Our discussion continued all the way back to Chicago. I felt that there was something more behind our harrowing experience. Bob, on the other hand, felt that the experience was nothing more than what it was—a to-be-expected imperfection in a mechanically driven device. Nothing was settled when we arrived at our home several hours later.

Before collapsing exhausted into bed, we noticed that our housekeeper, Maria, had uncharacteristically left a book from one of our shelves on a bedside table. Bob playfully tossed the book to me and out of curiosity, I flipped it open to a random page and began reading. My jaw dropped to the floor as I gaped with astonishment.

The "random" story I read, in the book my housekeeper had mistakenly forgotten to return to the bookshelf, was about a woman pilot in World War II. She was carrying seventeen servicemen aboard a twin-engine plane in which one engine, and then the other engine, stopped within a few seconds of takeoff. Failing to follow procedures, her copilot somehow turned the plane around, dodging telephone wires and poles, and landed it safely on the ground. He told her later that he heard a voice and that it had commanded to him every safety measure to take. The book went on to say that the chances of both engines going out on a twin-engine plane were one in 10 million.

I told Bob about the story I had encountered by chance. He reasoned that the odds of anyone experiencing a one in 10 million occurrence in the morning of a given day and then randomly reading about the exact same occurrence that evening were incalculable. His denial was broken, but his questions were only beginning. "What do you think God's trying to tell us?" he asked.

In the face of disaster, whether personal or global, we awaken to what really matters. I believe, as does Bob, that God wants us to know that, because life is fragile, it is precious—meant to be lived fully every minute and celebrated as often as possible. Whether it is Y2K reminding us to be prepared, or people helping each other to financial independence, we must value the life we are given.

We need to become more aware of the love that surrounds us in our daily lives, focus more attention on our sense of camaraderie and community spirit, and develop a deeper sense of awe and respect for the God-given gift of life. If we choose, we can deny God's presence in our day-to-day lives. But in the final analysis, it becomes abundantly clear that His is a presence we simply cannot deny and must not take for granted.

SAHARA:
THE FRUITFUL VOID

★

Roger Housden

Creaky old stairs they were, the ones leading up to the priest's flat; oak stained dark, lit at the top by a dim light seeping through one of those frilly lampshades fashionable in the fifties. Sister Paula was leading the way. She was the guest sister at Twymawr Convent in Wales. She pushed back the door at the top of the stairs and showed me the room. One wall was lined with bookshelves; on a table in the corner stood an electric kettle, a jar of instant coffee, and some tea bags. Along another wall, the one with the wooden crucifix nailed to it, was a single bed covered with a pink flock bedspread.

"You are most welcome to use the library." Sister Paula beamed a matronly grin.

"Thank you. I have brought my own books."

It was too late already to bite my tongue. She meant no harm—was simply the caring guest sister—but I was wary, on my guard. This was the first Anglican establishment I had set foot in since my childhood. I was thirty years old, but already the taste and feel of the place were evoking images from my youth: the obsequious local vicar, the social hierarchy, the self-conscious hymn singing, the drone of the sermon no one listened to. All so painfully bereft of passion, spirit, and meaning. Not just anxiety but arrogance had fueled my response. There could hardly be much of interest there for me on those dusty bookshelves lined with fading tomes on saints and church history.

She backed out of the room and left me gazing over the convent lawn to the single oak tree at the far end. Under the tree several plain wooden crosses stood to the memory of sisters who had lived and died at Twymawr. I had come there for a week because I wanted time for reflection at a period in my life when events were moving fast. The environment of a contemplative community seemed an ideal context, especially since I had been told I could follow my own schedule.

I had not accounted for the way a place can seep into the pores: the smell of the furniture, the view from the window, the bells, the frankincense that came floating up through the floorboards from the vestry below. I had not bargained for what I would find when, on the second day, unable any longer to resist the lure of the incense and the soft singing voices, I found myself stepping down the stairs to compline, the last service of the day. The chanting of the nuns, the presence they summoned, and their quality of attention evoked an unusual beauty, whose effect stayed with me as I walked back up the oak stairs after the service and sat in the chair facing the bookshelves.

I drew closer and surveyed the books lining the wall. In among the more predictable titles was a slim paperback by an author of whom I had never heard before: *Letters from the Desert* by Carlo Carretto. I picked it out, and by the time I had reached the last page, two hours later, I knew I was going to the Sahara, and soon. It wasn't a wish, it didn't even feel like a decision; it was a simple fact, no explanation needed, to myself or anyone else. Carretto had been a well-known Catholic activist in Italy when, at the height of his political and religious authority, he left everything to become one of the Little Brothers of the Desert, a renunciate order in the Sahara. His book filled me with the great gold and yellow spaces, and showed me how the desert can return a man to essentials. Reading his book, I realized how I wanted that, and also how much I wanted the raw color and the wildness of the desert. Not long afterward, I was on a plane to Algeria.

My love of the desert, then, began in a Welsh convent. In the summer of that same year I was on my way to Algeria, fired by a dream. My plane touched down at Tamanrasset airstrip in darkness. Tam was a tiny settlement then, in southern Algeria, not so far from the border with Mali. I spent the couple of hours before dawn in the little passenger building, talking to a moun-

tain of a man with a handlebar mustache who was on his way to
Chad to hunt rhinoceros. As the rocks began to glimmer in the
first light of dawn, I clambered into the Jeep that was to take us
to town. We bumped down the track, and within a few moments
the Sahara was unveiled to my staring eyes: a vast rolling moon-
scape of red rock and dust, streaked with the purple and yellow
of the emerging day. The sun that was rising over the farthest
crags was larger than any sun I had ever seen. As it lifted itself
higher into the gaping sky, the rocks burned redder and stood in
stark relief against the canvas of blue.

The flight from London to Algiers had taken us the same distance as the flight from Algiers to Tamanrasset. The second
flight, though, was over nothing but desert. The Sahara accounts
for a quarter of the entire continent of Africa and is widening its
borders every year. Tam is hundreds of miles from anywhere, in
the land of the Tuareg, a proud nomadic people who still fail to
recognize the arbitrary national borders across their territory. In
1975 Tam was a few streets of low houses, an old French cara-
vansary, and a fort—all constructed in adobe.

After a couple of days, I found an Arab guide who was willing to take me out into the desert and return for me three days
later. This was my dream: to know what it was like to be alone
out there, far from all trace of humanity. We rode out just as the
sun was rising and continued until early afternoon. We stopped
only for Said to dismount and say his prayers, and once to let the
camels nibble on a bush of thick leaves and thorns. For hours we
crossed a plain strewn with rocks and gullies. Mountains, some
as high as ten thousand feet, ringed the horizon. The desert was
more desolate, more sobering, than the Sahara of my imagination, yet more vibrant too, orange and red everywhere, with
streaks of black and purple shadow.

Finally, when we passed two slabs of rock that were leaning
against each other to form an open-ended cave, Said dismounted
and untied a goatskin of water from the camel's flank. This was
it then. Three days under two rocks in a sweltering plain. With
a faint smile of bemusement, Said rode off with our camels, back
along the ancient riverbed that we had been following for the
previous hour. As I watched him go, it occurred to me that I had

never before put myself so trustingly—so unthinkingly—into another's hands.

He disappeared over a slight rise, and I turned to contemplate my surroundings. No wind, no trace of movement, no sound; everything just where it had been for centuries, or so it seemed, illuminated by an unfiltered glare. Yet the heat, muted by an altitude of a few thousand feet, was bearable, even in high summer. Gooseflesh ran along my arm. I laid my bedroll between the rocks, heard my breathing, and felt the air pass an electricity through me. Never had I been so tangibly aware of my own existence. I wanted to sing out, but the immensity of the space took all sound away from me. The rest of that day I sat beneath the rock in awe, with a sheer animal joy, not just at the world to which I had come but also at the marvel of my own living and breathing.

Within a day it was all rather different. The drama and excitement of acting out a cherished daydream had evaporated. No longer was I playing the lead in some movie. There I was, alone in the midst of this desolate landscape, awoken each morning at the first glimmer of light by a swarming horde of buzzing bees, churning out the same ordinary thoughts as I did back in London. Their triviality, my own mundanity, stood out starkly in the desert glare. I found myself beginning to laugh. I was no great visionary or ecstatic; there was nobody particularly special hiding beneath my daily round waiting to be revealed, no reserved destiny or Damascus experience waiting to proclaim itself on the desert stage. No, beneath the ticktock of my hopes and fears, past and future, there was nothing to speak of at all—simply a sense of clear and empty space.

On my last day alone I walked out far from my rock into the empty expanse. After some while I stopped and looked back over the way I had come. I seemed to have walked no distance at all. My footprints had already been filled by the shifting sand, and there was no evidence of the effort I had made to come this far. Suddenly, there in the implacable light, I was stripped of all self-preoccupation and artifice. I was bared to an awareness of the deep insignificance of the personal melodrama that I had imagined to be my existence. In that moment, the emptiness without shone as a mirror for the spaciousness within; the living desert became a picture of my own innate condition. Standing there, a speck on a vast canvas, I felt true, authentic, and unashamedly small, without even a story to tell.

When Said appeared on the morning agreed, it felt so ordinary it was as if nothing had happened. In a way nothing had, and everything had. Bobbing up and down on that camel to Tam, I felt profoundly at peace with the world and with myself. No ecstasy, no revelation, just the smile of being at home.

A FARMER'S ADVICE

George R. Noory

One night a caller by the name of Jim phoned in to my talk radio show since we were discussing various mystical topics. He related a personal story:

"I was once very depressed; everything in my life was not going well. My job wasn't what I wanted, I had broken up with my girlfriend, and a number of other things had me extremely upset.

"It was a pretty November day in Missouri, so, despite my depression, I got into my car and just drove, trying to clear my head. Eventually, I came to a small town and saw a park bench next to a small lake and park. I got out and sat there for a while.

"While I was there, a farmer in old coveralls came by and sat next to me. Gus was a delightful person, and we chatted for an hour about the world in general and my problems in specific. His advice made me realize how important my life truly was. Afterwards, my depression was completely gone. I thanked him, and Gus wandered away. I got into my car and drove home.

"About a year later, after things had turned around for me, I decided to go back to that small town and thank the farmer. When I arrived, I did what most city folks would do—go to the local barbershop. I asked if the barber knew where I could find Gus.

"The barber replied, 'Best you talk to his daughter.' He pointed out where she lived.

"Sensing the worst, I knocked on the door. A woman answered, and I explained who I was, what her father had done for me, and asked if he was there. She said no—her father had died. But I was the fifth person to come by asking for his help and advice—even though her father, Gus, had died fifteen years ago!"

SAVED BY A VOICE

George Wrigley

As a pilot and flight instructor, I had had the dream and ambition in life to own and pilot a P51 Mustang, that beautiful World War II fighter aircraft. It's the ultimate in a propeller-driven airplane; it's sleek, fast, and gorgeous. However, since they cost several million dollars, I didn't have very high hopes of realizing this dream.

One day I saw, on the cover of an experimental aircraft magazine, a replica of the grand P51. This plane was made of wood and fabric, much like the airplanes in the early part of this century, but resembled a P51 in every other way. Maybe I could have my P51 after all, even if it wasn't the real thing. It sure looked like the real thing.

Several years went by, and I forgot all about my dream of owning the Mustang. My life had changed totally. I had gotten divorced, remarried, and moved from New England to Arizona. But because of my love of flying, I always kept current on my medical certificate and flying abilities. Then I saw it. It was in a neighbor's yard. The exact P51 Mustang I had seen years earlier on the magazine cover. I checked it out; the man who owned it had traded a car for it. But he didn't have a pilot's license to fly it. He really wanted an ultralight that didn't require a license to fly. And I just happened to have an ultralight. A deal was struck, and at last I had my P51 Mustang.

Upon inspecting the airplane, I found that the workmanship was not up to my standards. I set out to totally rebuild the airplane. This process took over three years, but when I finished I had what I thought was the most beautiful P51 replica ever.

After I got it to the airport, I couldn't wait to fly it. I attached the wings to the fuselage, hooked up the control cables, and everything appeared to work fine. As I was putting on the final hatch, the one that covered the access hole to the controls, I heard a voice, so loud and clear that I turned to see who was talking to me. But there was no one there, and I realized the voice was coming from inside me. It said, "You had better check the control cables."

I replied, "I've done that several times." And I continued putting the screws into the hatch.

Then I heard the voice again. And this time it was very loud and adamant. "Then you had better do it again!"

Upset over the delay in test-flying my new airplane, I replied, "Oh, all right!" I removed the hatch and threw the tools on the ground. "See. See," I said as I moved the control stick more vigorously than I had ever done from that vantage point. Then I saw it. When the control stick moved forward, which from inside the airplane would be back toward the pilot—the exact position needed for takeoff—the cables jammed into the wing ribs. The holes in the wing ribs were not nearly large enough to accommodate the back-and-forth motion of the control stick. I froze in horror. Had I flown the aircraft that way, surely I would have been killed.

"I'm sorry, God" was all I could say. "I didn't mean to yell at you. Thank you. Thank you, God."

I spent the rest of the day making the holes in the wing ribs big enough to accommodate the stick movement. When I finally finished and began to put the hatch on again, I listened very carefully, but no voice came. I test-flew the airplane, and the controls worked just fine. In fact, I flew that airplane for over a year before selling it.

In our society, it's okay to talk to God, but people who claim God talks to them are considered insane. I am not insane. More than once I have heard the voice of God or His angels. And I have learned to listen and to pay heed.

LESSONS IN ENGLISH

★

Mary Lennon

"No, I'm sorry, we have nothing available."
That's all I heard after two hours of trying to get a hotel room in England. What's more, I was doing this from a pay phone in France, and I was running out of options. I'd been in Europe for about three weeks. Some of the trip was wonderful, but a lot of it was frustrating, and it was a daily battle to find accommodations.

My absolute favorite thing to do on this trip was to go into the churches and light candles. I'd been to churches all over Venice, Italy, and to numerous churches in France. England was to be my last stop. I didn't have a huge pull to go there, France was my country. But it was a long-held dream of my mother's to go to England. She had loved anything and everything English as long as I could remember. We always had *Masterpiece Theatre* on our TV in suburban Minnesota. I knew who Glenda Jackson was before I knew of Meryl Streep. My mother adored the tradition, the fierce attention to language, the impeccable manners, the gardens, the furniture, everything of the English. All she ever wanted in life was to go to England. We never had the money growing up to travel, and then time ran out. She died a very brutal death due to cancer. I remember her being almost skeletal and looking at brochures, still trying to figure out a way. Stopping in England would be a way of honoring my mother.

I finally scored a hotel room, and I would be on the way in the morning. I took the Chunnel, which was semifreaky, but worse than that were the English customs agents. I was highly suspicious to them because I was a musician, there for only one night. This one woman questioned me like I was going to personally try to kick Prince Charles in the shins. Between that and the hotel battles, so far my impression of the English was one of complete underwhelm.

With one day to see all the sights, the challenge was obvious. Piccadilly Circus, check. Ride a double-decker, check. Big Ben, check. The Thames, the Tower of London, the Old Globe, check, check, check. I'd been pounding around on feet that'd been too tired, too sore for three weeks. The only thing I wanted to see for myself, and not just for my mother, was Kensington Palace, Princess Diana's home. I made it to the gate, the one we all saw on TV buried in a sea of flowers the summer before. There were still flowers, such beautiful letters, and poems on the gate, moving back and forth with the breeze. There was also a wave of grief there that simply flows through your marrow instantly; it buckles your knees. I found I really couldn't stand there very long; quite literally, it was so powerful I had to leave.

I was wiped out, burnt out on history, tradition, different cultures; I'd taken too much in. I was officially an American-fried tourist.

Going back to my hotel, I saw there was a church next to Kensington Palace. I had no desire to go into it. I'd seen enough, my feet ached, and I was ready to go home. I'd lit enough candles to cover me for a lifetime. Still there was a pull—an incredible pull—and I went in against my own will.

It was a beautiful church, breathtaking, as most European churches are. The quiet was heaven, and in a pew I saw a mother and daughter praying. I lit a candle, of course (what's one more?), but still couldn't figure out the pull of this church; it didn't seem unique to me.

Then, as I went to put a coin in the box for a donation, it dropped and fell on a ledge with a plaque in front of it. The plaque read: CHURCH OF MARY AT ST. GEORGE.

My name is Mary.

My mother's name was Georgeann. They had called my mother George for short; she was named after her grandfather.

The Church of Mary at St. George. Maybe it was angels, but I'm convinced it was my mother who drew me in it. She found the one church in all of Europe that included us both in its name, and I felt her presence right there, right with me. Finally she was in England. *We* were in England. In that space her spirit felt happy to me, maybe even young again. The image that had stayed with me, of her longing to go, was settled somehow.

I took a few minutes, just to breathe and take in the silence of the church. Then, before leaving through the door, I turned and saw the candle, with its small but beautiful flame, flicker as a drop of wax rolled down its side.

LONG DRIVE HOME

Julie Isaac

During the early eighties I worked part-time as a journey-man mailer at *The Denver Post*. Often pulling night duty, I would drive home at three or four in the morning, when the five-mile drive usually took fifteen to twenty minutes—unless it snowed.

One Saturday night in March, a foot and a half of snow had been predicted overnight. Relieved to hear the radio report that it had stopped snowing with only eight inches on the ground, I still was anxious to be on my way home. After the presses stopped and the last bundle of Sunday papers slid down the mail chute, our supervisor yelled, "Go home!"

It was three-fifteen on a Sunday morning. The snowplows wouldn't be out for hours.

I warmed up my nine-year-old Pinto wagon and cautiously pulled out onto Broadway; the snow was so deep only a slight dip distinguished sidewalk from street. My snow tires were virtually useless as I crawled along; my speedometer barely registered any speed at all. I caught every red light, and each step required a rolling start, with occasional trips to the trunk for old newspapers to provide additional traction.

Only halfway home after an hour, I took several long, deep breaths to relax. Another hour brought me within a mile of home. At a quarter after five neither snowplows nor church-goers were yet on the road. I hadn't seen another car pass in either direction for over forty-five minutes.

As I slowly inched my way home, the snow brought me to a halt once again. As I had done innumerable times in the last two hours, I backed up a few feet, then rolled forward, pushing gently on the accelerator. Only this time the car jerked violently as it came to an abrupt stop, wheels whirring like a blender. I tried to roll back but didn't move. I turned off the ignition, my eyes filling with tears. I was out of newspapers.

I struggled to remain calm while considering my options. I could walk home; it wasn't that far. But I had dressed to get from my front door to the car and back again, not for a mile hike in fifteen-degree weather. The steel-toed boots that protected me from harm at work might turn my toes into ice cubes when submerged in eight inches of snow. I could stay in the car and wait for the snowplows to come, but, it being Sunday, they might not be out for several more hours. Beginning to panic, I realized that if ever there were a time for prayer, this was it.

At various times in my life I have pleaded with God, begged for miracles, longed for grace, asked for help—but not this time. My prayer was as hard as the knot in my stomach: "You have to help me, God. I can't deal with this. I need your help and you will help me."

Too scared to risk my request being declined, I left God no options. I needed help and God *would* provide. Period. End of prayer.

Shocked by my own demand, I sat as several minutes passed until, in the distance, the sound of a car crawling across the snow broke the agonizing silence. A dark-colored Buick, driven by a sandy-haired young man, pulled up beside me. He rolled down his window; I rolled down mine.

"Are you all right, ma'am?" he asked with a reassuring smile.

The knot in my stomach began to unwind. I explained that my car was okay, but I needed traction to get unstuck. Without hesitation he jumped out of his car, pulled pieces of cardboard from his backseat, and placed one in front of each of my rear tires.

It worked.

He apologized for not being able to see me safely home, but his wife was waiting to be picked up and he was already late. Then he wished me a safe journey and drove off. Thankful and relieved, I watched his taillights disappear ahead of me.

After driving two blocks, I stopped for a red light. When my foot hit the accelerator, again, nothing happened. Unable to move backward or forward, I started to cry. I couldn't believe that God would send someone to my rescue only to let me get stuck again. Was this punishment for demanding help rather than asking for it?

Confused and scared, I decided to let go this time, to trust rather than demand. So I sat back and watched as the dawn slowly sketched the outlines of trees, houses, and the road ahead. Soon light began to fill in the details. As I saw my condo complex in the distance, the tension rushed out of my body. Ten minutes later I spotted another car heading in my direction. A dark car. A Buick.

"I was worried about you," he said, with that same reassuring smile, "so we came back to see if you made it home okay." His wife waved hello.

"Not quite, I'm afraid." Amazed by his generous spirit and God's protecting grace, I thanked him with words unable to reach the depth of my gratitude. Again he placed cardboard under my tires, enabling me to continue on my journey. Still inching my way through the snow, I felt Spirit riding with me this time. Finally, I made it home.

That five-mile drive took over three hours and did twelve hundred dollars' worth of damage to my car's engine. Yet what I remember most about that night is that grace rode with me, seeing me safely home. Grace and a wonderful man named Jim, who came to my rescue twice on that long drive home.

FACING DEATH ON KILIMANJARO

Sally M. Veillette

Why am I so drawn to climbing this mountain? The last mountain I climbed was seven years ago—Mount Rainier, in my home state of Washington. Mount Rainier is 14,410 feet high and a technical climb. Our group had used crampons, ropes, and ice axes to reach the summit. Kilimanjaro is different. At 19,340 feet, it stands almost a full mile taller than Rainier. The route we are taking is eight days long, compared to Rainier's two. It's a more gentle climb but to a significantly higher height.

Now, sitting here the night before I leave for Africa, single at age thirty-seven, I wonder why I feel so strongly that I have to write a will. To whom am I going to leave my things? My cat? Something inside of me is telling me that I am going to die up there on that mountain. And it is using very strong words. So I continue with my work, leaving the will in an obvious place and all my affairs in order.

As I board the flight to Africa, I feel like I'm stepping over the edge of a cliff. When we arrive the six Americans who form the climbing team jump into the back of a Jeep to go to the hotel that will be our home for the night. Rain starts to pour so heavily that I decide to pull out my new video camera and see if it will pick up the image in the dark, knowing that the combination of the darkness and the sound of the rain will form an auspicious beginning to my memories.

At the start of the climb, we can't even see the summit. We climb for two days, in fact, before we get our first brief view of Kilimanjaro through the clouds that cover the peak. It still looks so far away, we think to ourselves. Then someone says it out loud. Soon there are five days of climbing behind us. We are at the Arrow Glacier Camp, at about sixteen thousand feet. Those of our group who are unused to climbing mountains have felt the strain; I have not. Although I am standing at a place higher than I've ever stood before, our approach has been so gentle as to be surprisingly easy. We still have over three thousand feet to climb. I sense my time is yet to come.

The porters wake us early in the morning for the ascent up the Western Breach. Cleverly keeping the difficulty of the day ahead from us, they lead us, bit by bit, up the dangerous avalanche shoot. This Danger Zone, as they call it, is famous for hurling large rocks—rocks that have been loosened by the heat of the morning sun—down upon unsuspecting climbers. We are still in the Crazy Zone, the region of altitude sickness, the elusive illness that affects some climbers while leaving others untouched.

Researchers have little to say about why this illness strikes. Our guides are on a constant watch for its signs. For you can die from altitude sickness. Your brain can swell, and you can die. Our guide knows this all too well, for the day before he met us at the airport, he'd attended a funeral for another guide—someone who'd been up the mountain over twenty times before—who'd died of altitude sickness. But he keeps this to himself. All our guide tells us is that above sixteen thousand feet is the Crazy Zone. The oxygen is at half the level to which we are used, the air pressure much less. And strange things can happen.

My symptoms begin soon after arriving at the Summit Camp, 18,500 feet. I have a dull headache and really don't feel much like eating dinner. I throw a few noodles on my plate and drink down a bowl of soup. Our team is quiet—both tired from climbing over large boulders and loose scree, and in nervous anticipation of spending the night on top of the world. That night, we judge, is going to be the toughest part of the climb. I try to call my parents from our satellite phone, but they aren't home. So I call my sister, Jeanne. She says something that triggers a deep emotional reaction from me. She tells me she believes in me. She knows I'm going to make it.

I'm not sure why, but I start to cry. Perhaps I am feeling the true force of emotions, I surmise. Perhaps the extra air pressure at sea level helps you keep the lid on the box of your feelings. Lid off, insides exposed, a deep fear begins to overtake me. It heightens my altitude sickness, making me question what in the world I am doing there, wondering whether I will get to the top or not. Wondering if now is the time I am going to die.

Suddenly, in a confusing contrast, sweet memories of the week the team and I spent in Africa before the climb flash through my mind. The songs that serenaded our every move. The smiling faces of the desperately poor children. The village man who was wearing an inside-out pants leg as a hat. The complete joy, the total lack of self-consciousness. I hadn't realized how self-conscious I was until I'd felt the lack of it.

The fears, the memories, the tiredness of my body—my head pounds as an ache fills it to capacity. Soon I throw up in the sands near the twenty-story glacier that guards our camp. I find it hard to stop crying. The guides are concerned because I am the strong one, the one they'd never worried about before. But now they check my vital signs, then put me in a sleeping bag in their tent and watch me as I drift off to sleep.

I awake some time later relieved that my symptoms are waning slightly. Then a wave of fear rises up once again, instantly magnifying my symptoms. The guides reassure me, and I return to sleep. Soon I wake up again. My symptoms are less, the fear a little quieter, the sleep just that much easier to resume.

This continues six or seven times through the night. And each time I feel a wave of energy lift off of me—a deep, tingling sensation, a feeling I'd had before but only when working with healers. By morning I am free of all symptoms, all fears, and I am ready for the one-and-a-half-hour climb to the top.

As we prepare ourselves to leave the summit, pictures having been taken, hugs exchanged, I realize that something in me has, indeed, died on this mountain. Old fears have left my heart, as if the karmic remnants of a hundred lifetimes have been freed at last. I feel a peace like I've never known before, a renewed contact with the richness of life, the unconscious impediments no longer getting in the way.

A new flow has opened within my body—fearless, worryless,

both strong and gentle at the same time. I am full, more whole, fueled by the energy of the moment. As I continue down the steep mountain trail, I feel as if I am born again and that each moment is a new friend to me. I realize it is not my job to control my moment, to try to make it a happy one. It is my job to live it, no matter what it brings. To feel each part of each moment—its happiness, its sadness, its elations, its frustrations.

In the moment, I cannot pretend to be something I'm not; I cannot pretend to like something or someone I don't. I cannot deceive myself, even a tiny bit. I am only me—and all me.

I laugh to myself at the thought of my will sitting on my counter at home. It seems that, indeed, another person had drafted it.

BLIZZARD
HOUSECLEANING

★

Stephen J. Hopson

We were on our way from New York to Michigan and had driven seven hundred miles without incident when my friend and I decided to stop at a gas station in a tiny rural town of Canada. It was time for coffee and a quick trip to the bathroom. Climbing out of the car, I looked up at the sky. It was dark and ominous, almost foreboding. The air was uncomfortably damp, and it was drizzling lightly.

I went to the rest room and scurried back to the car. Even though the gas tank was only half-empty, I felt it best to refill it. Normally, I would wait until the fuel gauge flashed me a warning sign. However, I filled it up, paid for it with a credit card, and hurried back to the freeway.

To my delight, it began to snow. But in the blink of an eye, it swirled down harder and harder, sharply reducing visibility. In a matter of minutes it was nightfall, and I was forced to slow the car to a crawl. My stomach tightened for the first time that night.

Roads were fast turning to ice, and the wind blew harder with each passing minute. It felt as if I were piloting a small aircraft through severe turbulence. We had to find a hotel, quickly.

Eventually my friend and I saw what we both thought was a sign for hotel accommodations right before an exit. The blinding storm made it difficult for us to see it clearly, but we decided to take the chance and got off the freeway.

About a mile down the road, we spotted a lone car up ahead of us. Thinking they were from the area, we followed them, but after a few minutes we realized they were lost too. We had no choice but to go back the other way.

Turning the car around on the narrow two-lane road was no easy feat. The wind was howling menacingly all around us. The possibility of being windswept into the ditches was real—very real. With the greatest concentration I could muster, I took a deep breath and swung the car back and forth, inches at a time, to turn around. Suddenly the rear wheels spun like crazy.

It was a sickening feeling. Despite the danger of sinking even deeper into the snow, I continued to rock the car until the wheels finally caught on and the car miraculously lurched forward.

Thank God.

We went the other way, my heart pounding wildly. There was no sign of life in the ghostly white landscape. My friend convinced me to get back on the freeway and perhaps find an overpass for temporary shelter until the storm blew over.

I looked at the gas meter. Incredibly it was still *full*.

Hunching over the steering wheel and squinting my eyes, I tried to see through the howling blizzard to find the ramp, but it was nearly impossible to see where I was going.

In the midst of all this, somehow I remembered I was carrying in my right pocket a small stone with FAITH inscribed across the surface. My right hand shook as I reached down to touch the smooth, polished rock. Wrapping my hand around the stone, I closed my eyes and pleaded, "Dear God, please get us back on the freeway. Please guide us home now."

As I opened my eyes, my mouth dropped in astonishment. We had made it to the freeway entrance! How we got there, I'll never know.

Clutching the steering wheel, I slowly drove up the icy ramp, completely relying on the small yellow reflectors shimmering in the glare of the car's headlights. We continued the treacherous journey, driving at a snail's pace for the longest time.

I breathed a sigh of relief when we saw several beams of light in the distance, resembling a small, bustling city. But as we got closer we saw it wasn't a city—it was a bunch of cars and trucks stuck in the ditches with their headlights illuminating and crisscrossing the snowy night sky! All we could do was pray for them as we drove on in stunned silence.

At this point past and current problems totally vanished from my mind. I found myself mentally forgiving everyone who had "wronged" me in the past. I released all my resentments, anger, and ego-related issues to God. My biggest concern that night was to get home *alive*. Never before had I done so much mental housecleaning in one night!

Nine hours later our weary, bleary eyes saw the most beautiful sign we had ever seen. It said: BRIDGE TO USA, 27 MILES. Tears rolled down my face as we finally drove across the border. We were home.

Who says God doesn't know how to give you a good cause for mental housecleaning?

He even paid for the gas. The charge never showed up on my credit card.

ANGELS: DON'T LEAVE HOME WITHOUT THEM

★

Doreen Virtue, Ph.D.

I travel for a living, giving weekend seminars across North America. I've learned through experience that angels make wonderful traveling companions. They help to smooth the way and untangle travel plans.

The angels taught me, with their unique brand of humor, the importance of asking for help in every situation. It happened when my husband, Michael, and I were in Scottsdale, Arizona, during one of my seminars. Our Arizona hosts dropped Michael and me off at a health club in North Scottsdale on Saturday night. They offered to pick us up later, but Michael and I said we'd take a cab back to our hotel.

Following our workout, Michael used the health club's phone and yellow pages to call a cab company. The first taxi dispatcher said, "Oh, we don't service North Scottsdale." The second cab company said they weren't familiar with the street our gym was located on. A third taxi company said, "Well, we're very busy tonight, so it might take us forty or fifty minutes to get out there."

Dejected, Michael and I decided to walk to our hotel. After all, we rationalized, we'd both just spent time on a treadmill; what was another hour of exercise? Still, we realized it would be a difficult trek. For one thing, there were no sidewalks and we were on very uneven, rock-laden dirt in the dark. Tripping and stumbling, we decided to search the busy street next to us for a taxicab or bus.

The fifty-mile-an-hour traffic whizzed by, with no sign of any public transportation. Too residential a neighborhood for buses and taxis, Michael concluded aloud.

I groused silently to my angels. "How come you guys let me down after I gave my all today, teaching people about you angels? I did my part, how come you're not helping us with a taxi?"

At that moment I heard the angels' sweet but wry inner reply: "Excuse me, but did you ask us to get you a cab?"

I gasped in realization. I hadn't asked the angels to get me a taxi. No wonder Michael and I were having such difficulty. We were trying to take care of everything from a human level!

"Consider this my official request right now, dear angels," I mentally replied. "Please send us a taxi, right away!" I explained my angelic conversation to Michael, and we both realized that help was at hand.

Not more than two minutes later, I turned around in time to see a big, brand-new yellow cab in the lane next to us driving about thirty miles an hour. I reached my hand out, as if hailing a New York cab. The driver pulled over immediately. Michael, I, and the angels smiled as the taxi driver comfortably took us to the hotel. On the way he mentioned that it was a fluke for him to be driving on our street. "Cabs normally don't service this residential area at all," he said nonchalantly as Michael and I winked knowingly at each other.

Since that incident I remember more often to involve my angels with every aspect of my life. They have taught me that they are not allowed to intervene without our express approval.

I'm on airplanes nearly every weekend, giving workshops in one to two cities. Flying this much would usually mean encountering a percentage of problems, but when you bring your angels along on trips, the statistics are more in your favor.

Because of the storms around the country, the Atlanta airport was practically shut down one Sunday night when I, and thousands of other travelers, were trying to catch flights. The only airline that was flying was Delta; all the other carriers canceled their flights. So everyone was pouring into the Delta terminal, struggling to get airline seats.

The Delta plane that I initially boarded for Los Angeles sat on the tarmac for thirty minutes. Then the pilot announced that, because of mechanical problems, the flight was canceled and we'd all have to leave and try to get seats on other flights.

We returned to the terminal amid a sea of people standing at a gate podium, demanding to be allowed on the only remaining flight in the airport going to California. Again I prayed and asked the angels to help me get home. I was tired and had clients to see the next day. Somehow, the crowd pushed me to the front of the line.

The flight had only a limited number of seats remaining, and hundreds were vying for them. Several people were screaming at gate attendants, demanding a seat on the plane. It poignantly reminded me of the scene in the movie *Titanic* where people fought for lifeboat seats.

I began talking with a couple in front of me in line. We smiled and joked, while nervously noticing the many people who were mobbing the ticket counter. I felt that we were in the eye of a volatile hurricane. Then it was my new friends' turn at the gate. The ticket agent said to them, "I've got three seats left on the plane. They're all in the rear of the plane, but they're yours if you want them."

The ticket agent looked at me and then turned back to the couple and asked, "Is this person traveling with you also?"

"Yes, she is," the couple replied. Moments later, as I sank into my seat, which was miraculously an aisle seat, I thanked God, the angels, and the couple profusely for helping me so gently and easily.

Another time Michael and I were walking to the baggage claim area to get our four big suitcases filled with supplies for my workshop. It was late on a Friday night, and we were hungry for dinner.

I said to Michael, "Let's ask Raphael, the archangel of healers and travelers, to get the luggage off the plane right away." I then hesitated, because I knew the importance of being careful what you ask for. If you're going to specify to the angels what you want, you better make sure to fill in all the blanks of your request carefully. So I edited my request to Raphael, "I don't mean for you to get the luggage so quickly that the suitcases fall onto the tarmac. Just please have them be on the luggage carousel right away."

I thought I was covering all of my bases with this request, but the angels taught me how they take our requests literally. As I walked away from the carousel to rent a big luggage cart, I heard Michael's voice calling for help. I turned around and saw all four of our suitcases had come down the luggage chute simultaneously. Unfortunately, since they came out together, Michael couldn't grab them all at once. So we waited while our bags made their trip all the way around the large carousel at the international airport. We both thought of the same conclusion: Next time we'll be more careful of what we ask for!

THE EYE OF THE STORM

★

Cathy Adams

A couple of years ago my father took my sister and me fishing on the banks of a river. On the way we stopped and asked a man we met how we could get to the other side. It is remarkable how peaceful I felt just talking to the man. He was on a bicycle; that was the only thing we three all saw—besides his eyes—that we agreed later was the same. He had the most amazing, bright blue eyes we had ever seen. I got lost in them while he gave us our directions.

We were proceeding to fish on the riverbank when the man who had helped us suddenly appeared on the opposite shore. This river was quite wide and a little rough; therefore the waters were very noisy. Yet when he shouted out to us, "The eye of the storm is coming! The eye of the storm is coming!" we could hear him as if he were standing right next to us. It should have been impossible to make out his voice.

My dad immediately picked up all of his equipment like he was hypnotized and began walking to the car. My sister and I asked him where he was going, and he said, very calmly, that he had to go. He was acting strange. There was a steep cliff that we had to climb to get to the top of the riverbank; nonetheless he jumped up it, without any effort, and went straight to the car.

The two of us kept fishing for a few minutes, and the man across the river disappeared. It started pouring down rain in what soon became the biggest electrical storm I have ever witnessed. My sister and I grabbed our fishing poles and struggled up the cliff to run back to the car, where we saw our father sitting alone, staring out at us.

To get to the car we had to cross a field and pass through some trees. Next we had to cross a barbed-wire fence at the place the car was parked. Lightning started hitting the ground, too close for comfort, so we began running. As soon as my sister and I cleared the fence, lightning struck in the exact spot we had crossed it.

If we had been a second later, we would surely have been hit.

My dad just sat in the car in a daze. We jumped in and asked him what he was doing. He said that when the stranger told us the eye of the storm was coming, he knew he had to get to the car—and that's what he had done.

Later that evening we discussed the day's events and tried to figure out the whole thing. Each one of us had seen the man in a different light. I saw him barefoot, bare-chested, and wearing long cutoff shorts. My sister said he had on jeans and a T-shirt. My dad thought he had on brown pants and didn't recall if he had a shirt on or not.

We all noticed his blue eyes, though. They and the bicycle were only thing we all saw.

None of us had any idea how we could have possibly heard what he was saying to us from across the river. The water was much too loud and he was too far away to hear him so clearly. Still he was able to warn us in time to get away. It was amazing.

We believe the man was an angel. It made us so happy that night just to think about him. My family still gets together and talks about our fishing trip, which we remember like we shared some kind of dream. We can never forget that day or the man who warned us to get out of the storm.

HITCHHIKING IN EUROPE

★

Mary Ellen "Angel Scribe"

In my early twenties I was a switchboard operator for Chevron in Canada. I loved the job but knew deep within my soul that if I did not do something drastic, I would be working in this job for the next thirty years and regretting the passing of time . . . and my life. I gave two weeks' notice and bought an airplane ticket to Europe. I had no idea what I was going to do, where I was going, or why. I just knew in my soul that I had to go.

The trip was a spiritual awakening for me. In the great cathedrals of Europe the floors are not wooden boards, as in America, but stones carved and dedicated to deceased loved ones. You are literally standing on grave markers. This visual stepping-stone into the past lets you put your own life into perspective. As I gazed down at the stones, it was apparent that life passes all too quickly. People buried there had lived to the age of eighty-six, yet here they were lying beneath my feet two hundred years later.

When I was in Germany I met Nancy, an American. One day we were hitchhiking together to see the scenery of that beautiful country—everyone did it back then in Europe—and we were picked up in two separate U.S. Army trucks. The trucks were being delivered to a single location forty miles away. Nancy and I would return together after we were dropped off.

The driver of my truck had rather unethical plans. This young soldier from New York was a sexual predator, and he started to attack me. I was thinking as fast as I could to deter his advances. I told him that I was not that "kind" of woman. But he said he didn't care.

Just then a male voice, from an invisible source outside of my left ear but very audible to me said, "Tell him you will tell."

I thought that wouldn't work so I said, "How would you like

your sister to come to Europe and make love to all the men she meets?" I was thinking he would see that if she would not do that then neither was I that kind of young woman.

He responded, "She probably would."

I thought, Uh-oh.

The invisible male voice outside my left ear repeated, "Tell him you will tell."

I thought that idea was nuts and would not deter any attacker. The funny part now is that at the time I never considered it odd to have heard the voice. (Maybe if I had said "Do you hear that little voice?" the soldier would have thought I was crazy and left me alone.) I had a knife with me to cut my French bread and tomato sandwiches. So instead I threatened the soldier: "If you don't get me off me, I will pull my knife on you."

The soldier said, "That won't bother me." Then he pushed up his shirtsleeves and revealed knife marks all up and down his arms from New York street fights.

Again I thought, Uh-oh.

The male voice outside my left ear said, *"Tell him you will tell!"*

I thought, Shesh! If a knife won't work, why would that statement? But I had nothing left to say, so I said, "I will tell!"

Well, much to my surprise, the guy leaped off of me. I was so stunned. He said, "You wouldn't."

My brain was mulling it over. Here I am, in a country where I don't speak the language; I don't have anyone to call or to tell. I did not even know where we were. It was a ridiculous threat. Nonetheless, I said, "Yes, I will tell."

The soldier immediately started the truck and drove me in silence to the depot where the other truck was waiting with Nancy, who had been worried about me and was very glad to see me. I never told Nancy about the voice.

It is amazing how, often, we are afraid to share the gifts we get from God: the voices of the angels as they protect, inform, and guide us. Consider this. Maybe it is normal to hear such voices. Maybe it is normal to receive divine guidance. As we share our stories with others, fear leaves us and an understanding of the great mysteries and miracles of life unfolds. May this knowledge empower us all.

A STRANGER ON A BUS

★

Cory Hunter Olson

I was taking the Phoenix city bus to the southern part of town, thankful for a seat to myself. It was midwinter, and the sun was beaming in the side window across the aisle so that when I looked up the glare blinded me. As we stopped to pick up passengers, the first one up the stairs hauled a black garbage bag stuffed full with his worldly possessions. He was ragged and worn, and from three rows back I could tell he wouldn't be doing my nose any favors.

"Please, God," I begged. "Don't let him sit next to me."

He eased himself and his load down next to me. Immediately turning my way, his foul breath punching me in the face, he took my hand. "Good morning, Sister. Can I have a prayer with you?"

Before I could object his quiet prayer began in earnest. I squirmed. I wiggled. I wanted to smash the window and bolt, screaming. I couldn't climb over him; his bag and bulky knees imprisoned me. How would Mother Teresa or Jesus handle this one? Thanks a lot, God. You try sitting next to him.

I reclaimed my hand from his before his prayer ended. The grimy gloves on his hands were worn away at the fingertips. When I tried to sneak a look at his face while he prayed, the sun's glare prevented my seeing anything but a dark blob.

"Thank you for being so kind to me, Sister," he said when the prayer ended. "Can I hold your hand again?"

"No."

"You know, Jesus is alive today."

"Mm-huh."

"See that man over there? He's blind."

I cringed as he pointed at an old man with a cowboy hat and

a white cane sitting in the seat directly facing ours. Their knees were almost touching.

"He must have a hard time walking. I bet he falls on his face because he can't see, huh?" For some reason that thought made him chuckle.

Great. Not only is he filthy and smelly, but he's a nutcase, too. I wondered again about Mother Teresa and Jesus as I hoped the blind man might also be deaf.

"I'm sure he gets around pretty well," I replied, trying to head off a fight.

"Do you ever see Jesus?" I could tell he was looking at me as he asked this question, but the blazing sun prevented my looking in his direction. I wasn't quite sure how to answer him anyway.

Fortunately, my stop was approaching. As I hastily climbed over him and his burden, I stole a quick glance back at his face, smiling up at me. For the first time since he sat down I could see who he was. For one brief, startling moment, my eyes rested on the sweetest, gentlest, most beguiling countenance I have ever laid eyes on.

I scrubbed my hands thoroughly when I reached my destination. But the memory of his captivating face haunts me. About a week after that encounter I heard for the first time Joan Osborne's song "One of Us." In it she asks, "What if God was one of us, just a stranger on a bus?"

I've been wondering "what if" ever since.

THE REVEREND AL GREEN

Suzanne Rowe

It began as a trip to Graceland. My sister, Janice, and I decided to grant our brother David's "burnin' desire" to visit the home of his hero, Elvis. David, thirty-five years old with Down's syndrome, has always loved music and especially the King. So we packed up her seven-year-old son, Jack, grabbed her husband, Keith, left our homes in Detroit, and took a four-day weekend in Memphis.

I researched the trip ahead of time on the Internet and discovered that the Full Gospel Tabernacle, home to the Reverend Al Green, is only minutes from Graceland. Al Green has always been one of my musical heroes, and the thought of attending his church service on Sunday—the last day of our trip—was appealing because of my admiration for his hit songs "Love and Happiness," "Let's Stay Together," and "Tired of Being Alone," to name a few, not necessarily for his preaching. I have struggled to overcome my repulsion for the closed-mindedness of some organized religions.

Lately, however, I had been feeling a stirring of a new spirituality within myself, finding guidance and comfort from inner reflection. Perhaps this also led me to make the Full Gospel Tabernacle a part of our motley crew's itinerary.

Our family spent a full three days discovering Memphis, visiting sights, and touring Graceland. Sunday morning we loaded the rental van with our bags and souvenirs and followed the map to Hale Road and the church of the Reverend Al Green. Keith was driving, I was navigating, and David, Janice, and Jack were in the back. We found Hale Street easily enough. As we neared the next block, a small, unassuming church appeared in the distance. Seeing the words THE FULL GOSPEL TABERNACLE, PASTOR AL

GREEN on a stand-up sign in front brought a chill to my spine and an unanticipated surge of adrenaline to my body. Keith had to tell me to calm down. I certainly hadn't figured on that level of excitement.

We entered and took places in the back. Looking toward the altar, we saw musicians, a preacher at the pulpit, and lo and behold . . . the Reverend Al Green sitting in the front pew! A low and steady beat started from the band, and a wonderful blue-and-white-robed choir of twenty or so began to enter slowly from both sides behind us, swaying with the music and singing, "Stand! Stand! Stand!"

When the choir was in place at the back of the altar, the preacher began preaching and Reverend Al joined him in the pulpit. The ministers and congregation were testifying and dancing, and the choir was in full bloom. The music increased in intensity as two or three choir members shared the lead, singing alone and in tandem with the Reverend. Within a short time the whole room was in a passionate frenzy, voices calling out, people dancing in the aisles.

I turned and looked as David got up and began walking toward the back door. Nature was calling, and I thought I'd better help him find the men's room even though I hated to leave the service. A helpful staff member guided us to a hallway around the side of the church, where I stood outside the rest room waiting for my brother. From my vantage point close to the altar, I could hear the music and noticed people coming and going.

A beautiful robed woman from the choir approached me— she had sung one of the leads moments before—and welcomed me to their church. I will never forget what happened next. She took both of my hands in hers and asked if she could pray with me. Not knowing what to expect, yet not wanting to seem ungracious, I said yes. The woman looked in my eyes and began, "Sister, you are carrying too much within you. You are a chosen child of God. Let the Holy Spirit enter you and release this anguish and worry that you carry."

I felt a surge of electricity and power come up my spine. The pressure from my shoulders began to release and rush through my arms, traveling through my hands into hers. My head lowered, and tears were flowing from my eyes as she continued talking, quietly yet fervently. Something powerful was happening at that moment through her words, between the two of us and the power of God.

She said, "Raise your head." I looked into the eyes of an angel who was telling me to "feel strong, release your burdens, and trust that God is with you and will lead the way."

All I could say was "Thank you, Sister. Thank you, God." The previous two years had brought me many challenges: illness in the family, an out-of-state move and subsequent return, the contemplation of a new career, and on and on. Yet in that moment I felt the worry and stress leave me and I no longer felt alone with my burdens.

When she released my hands, I was still shaking. My new friend told me her name was Beverly and that she would like to see me after the service. Just then, with amazing timing, David came out of the men's room ready to return to our place in church. We slid into our pew, where Janice looked at me quizzically. After all, I had just been crying and I must have looked shaken up. She leaned over and said that we couldn't stay till the end of the service; we had to catch our plane and wouldn't have the time. So I never had the chance to meet up with Beverly.

Something spiritually wondrous happened that day. Since then many events have taken place that I know are guided by God. That moment in Memphis changed my life, and I am convinced, after all these years of searching, that I have finally found a spirituality that will guide me all my days.

A year later Al Green made a Detroit appearance at the Masonic Temple. Of course, Janice and I got our tickets early to make sure we'd get good seats. The night of the concert, with Janice in the lead, we rushed down to stand directly in front of the stage. After a while Al reached down and handed Janice a rose! How wonderful, I thought, with a little envy, of course. She returned to her seat while I remained. I, too, wanted a rose.

Moments later Al stopped singing in the middle of a song and said, "Excuse me for stopping, there is something I have to do." He then put the microphone down, walked over to where I was standing, bent down, took my hands, and kissed me. Out of thirty women or so, he had come over to me!

I believe that the Reverend Al Green and his angel, Beverly, are working very closely with God and bringing me a message. No one can tell me otherwise. Now it's up to me to accept this blessing and spread the Word.

CONTRIBUTORS

Steeped in the mythopoetic tradition of Jungian psychology, **Jeremiah Abrams** has worked for thirty years in the helping professions. His books include the best-selling *Meeting the Shadow: The Hidden Power of the Dark Side of Human Nature*, *The Shadow in America: Reclaiming the Soul of a Nation*, and *Reclaiming the Inner Child*. He is the director of the Mt. Vision Institute (www.mtvision.org), a certification counseling program in Marin County, California.

Cathy Adams may be contacted by e-mail at cathyadams5@hotmail.com.

Gail Albert is originally from Newport Beach, California. She and her husband currently live on the Sunshine Coast in Queensland, Australia, where she is a follower of Tibetan Buddhism and receives spiritual guidance and teachings through the Chenrizig Center for Buddhist Studies. A world traveler, she has had many unique adventures and, while her travels in Tibet are the highlight of her spiritual experience, she finds love and light wherever she goes. Gail has contributed articles to publications for the Betty Ford Center and the AIDS Project Los Angeles. She can be reached by mail at 2-21 Bluefin Court, Noosaville, Queensland, Australia 4556.

Sarabeth Archer is a freelance writer and actor living in the Northeast.

Kerry Louise Atlee lives in Sydney, Australia. Her e-mail address is kezalu@hotmail.com.

Gregg Braden is a bestselling author and guide to sacred sites throughout the world. A former earth scientist and senior computer systems designer (Phillips Petroleum, Martin Marietta aerospace, Cisco Systems), Braden is now considered a leading authority on the spiritual philosophy of the ancient Essenes and many indigenous traditions around the world. Reach him at ssawbraden@aol.com; or visit his Web site: www.greggbraden.net.

Pam Brown resides in Cincinnati with her husband, Wayne, and her children Brett and Shannon. Her son Philip lives on in her heart. She is the director of the Program Management Office at a health insurance company. She holds a B.S. in accounting from Centenary College of Louisiana and an M.B.A. in finance from Xavier University. You can reach Pam by e-mail at PamBrown@hehe.com.

Victoria Bullis is a psychic with over twenty years of professional experience. She is heard on over eighty radio stations throughout the United States, Canada, Hong Kong, New Zealand, Australia, and the United Kingdom. She has just finished her first book and contributes articles to magazines and newspapers. You can reach her by phone at 888-686-2200; e-mail at vicbullis@aol.com; or at her Web site: www.victoriabullis.com.

Peggy J. Cain was a philosophy major in college and has spent twenty years in metaphysical studies, which have led her to several parts of the country. She lectures on dreams and their meaning, is a published poet, and contributes to the *Daily Home Newspaper* in the advertising department. She is the mother of three children and has three grandchildren. She enjoys music and working in her rose garden.

Roger W. Clevenger was born and raised in Central Illinois, where he still resides with his wife of eleven years and their three children. A former factory worker, he took time off while recovering from a head injury to do some writing, a hobby he has dabbled in over the years. Roger writes from the heart about things he has experienced. You may contact him by e-mail at clevy328@excite.com.

Rik Cooke, a National Geographic photographer of many years, and his wife operate a retreat center on seventy-seven acres of the island of Molokai in Hawaii. This nonprofit center is dedicated to creativity, healing, and education through workshops. Rik can be contacted at 808-567-6430.

Maggie L. Cooper enjoys writing about the normal, paranormal, abnormal, and supernatural parts of life. In the past twelve years her articles, stories, and poems have appeared in numerous publications in Canada, Italy, and the United States, including *Catholic Digest, Sword of Shahrazad, Tales of the Twisted Side, Today's Family, Fate, Hauntings, Ghost Trackers Newsletter,* and *Hot Chocolate for the Mystical Teenage Soul.* She resides in Jacksonville, Florida, and is working on a book about cat ghosts. Her e-mail address is Maggiepage@aol.com.

Irina H. Corten, Ph.D., was born in Moscow, of a Russian mother and an American father. She holds a doctorate in Russian literature from the University of California at Berkeley. She is a professor at the University of Minnesota, where she teaches Russian language, literature, culture, and women's studies. Her scholarly publications include the book *Vocabulary of Soviet Society and Culture.* Apart from her academic career, she is a practitioner of shamanism and the author of numerous articles on this subject.

Mike G. Doty is a 1979 retiree from the United States Air Force, currently operating his own company, which designs and administers career progression and training systems for major industry. Mike and his wife, Nicki, spent most of the ten years following his time in the service outside the United States in business. Currently the Dotys reside in Edgewater, Florida. Mike can be contacted through his Web site, www.freeyellow.com/members2/smtsinc, or via e-mail at oracle388@aol.com.

Micki East, M.A., is a mother, counselor, writer, teacher, and professional speaker. Her biggest joy in life is her son, Alexsei. She is the site coordinator for mental health services in an elementary school-based program for children with emotional and behavioral problems.

Mary Ellen, known internationally as Angel Scribe, is a Canadian currently residing in Cottage Grove, Oregon. She is the author of *Expect Miracles* and *A Christmas Filled with Miracles* and creator of the on-line Angels and Miracles Good-News-Letter (www.angelscribe.com), which reaches an estimated fifty thousand readers worldwide. Mary Ellen's purpose is to uplift readers' hearts and souls to help them see the world with new eyes and to live more fulfilling lives. The images Mary Ellen creates enable her readers to "be in" her writings empathically. Her spiritual leadership comes from the heart. She can be reached by e-mail at MaryEllen@angelscribe.com, or write: P.O. Box 1004, Cottage Grove, OR 97424.

The Rev. Dr. Iris D. Freelander is associate pastor at Angelus Fellowship of Long Beach, California. Further occupied as a past life therapist and spiritual counselor, Iris is past president of Friends of Cedar House, Sandlarks, and is the founding member of Long Beach Youth Home Boosters.

His Royal Highness Prince Mark Gonzaga Castello De Medici is a guest lecturer on inspiration, attainment of goals, health, happiness, the human condition, and the spiritual dimension. You may contact him by mail: H.R.H. Gonzaga De Medici, 999 North Doheny Drive, West Hollywood, CA 90069. Proceeds from the publication of his story in *Magical Souvenirs* have been donated to the Save the Children Fund.

Stephanie Gunning is a freelance writer, editor, and actor living in New York City. Her stories have also been included in *More Hot Chocolate for the Mystical Soul, Hot Chocolate for the Mystical Teenage Soul, Hot Chocolate for the Mystical Lover,* and *Angel Visions*. You may contact her by phone at 212-802-7856 or by e-mail at stephgun@aol.com.

Donald D. Hartman is a retired educator who served as the foreign language coordinator for the Jefferson County Public School District in Birmingham, Alabama, and as an adjunct professor at the University of Alabama in Birmingham, where he taught foreign language methodology and linguistic theory at the master's and doctoral levels. Studies at the University of Tennessee and the University of the Americas in Mexico City yielded him a bachelor's degree, and he holds both a master's degree and an A.A. from the University of Montevallo. He has several professional publications to his credit and is the author of *The Lemurian Connection*.

Lacey Hawk is a novelist, poet, and screenwriter. Since early childhood she has been aware of the beauty and love that exist beyond this earthly plane. She began to experience communication with the spirit world before the age of five but kept it to herself until she was well into her thirties. Her first work, *Born of Betrayal,* has recently been adapted for the screen, and she has just finished her second screenplay. Her twenty-one-year-old son, Kurtis, resides in Las Vegas, Nevada.

Jessie Heller-Frank is an award-winning poet. Her writing includes a variety of genres, from creative nonfiction and journalism to children's books and poetry. Much of her work deals with her religious and cultural background as a Jew. Jessie can be contacted by e-mail at cheller@community.net.

After undergraduate art study at the University of Southern California, **Dr. Frances Heussenstamm** became a high school art teacher, then professor of art and education, first at California State University in Los Angeles and later at Columbia University. Her doctoral research concerned creativity and alienation, and she has published more than seventy articles in her fields. Eventually her interests led her to explore the individual and collective interior world, and she became a licensed clinical psychologist. Her most recent book, *Blame It on Freud: A Guide to the Language of Psychology,* was a commission published in 1993. A powerful dream led her back to painting, and she subsequently left private practice to spend four years in an art studio in Western Australia. She now lives in Dana Point, California. You may contact her by e-mail at fkheuss@cs.com.

Triana Jackie Hill is an internationally respected teacher and lecturer and has taught her Beyond Conception Empowerment Workshops in sixty-five countries. She is a multitalented clairvoyant, able to read the Akashic Records, which are the individual records of a soul's evolution through time. Her book, *Der unsichbare Liebhaber,* has been published in German-speaking countries, and she is soon to be published in the United States. Triana is a spiritual and business counselor listed in *Who's Who in American Women.* She has her own radio show, *Ask Triana,* and does TV and radio appearances around the globe. She can be reached at her company, Interlink Unlimited, P.O. Box 1988, Kihei, HI 96753; phone: 808-874-1888; fax: 808-874-8777; e-mail: link@mauigateway.com; Web site: www.mauigateway.com/link.

Stephen J. Hopson is an inspirational speaker and author. Profoundly deaf since birth, he is a risk taker with a capital *R.* In 1996 Stephen gave up his lucrative Wall Street career to pursue his divine calling as a speaker-author. At the time he hadn't spoken to a live audience since college (1978–1982), nor did he have any writing credentials. Today he is a popular keynote speaker, author of *Goodbye Wall Street!* and contributor to *Chicken Soup for the College Soul* and *Heartwarmers.* When people hear him speak, hearts open, minds are inspired, and bodies are motivated into action. To book or contact Stephen, fax 734-629-0480, e-mail sjhopson@attglobal.net, or visit his Web site: www.sjhopson.com.

Julie Isaac is a freelance writer living in Los Angeles. She has a degree in creative writing from San Francisco State University. Julie is also a singer who has performed with choirs in Los

Angeles and San Francisco, and has appeared in musicals produced by the Culver City Civic Light Opera.

Connie Kaplan is an author, spiritual guide, dream teacher, and urban mystic, cleverly disguised as a soccer mom. She is the author of *The Woman's Book of Dreams: Dreaming as Spiritual Practice.* She lives in Southern California with her regal consort and two master teachers, cleverly disguised as her husband and two children.

Kathleen Keith has been on a quest for spiritual information all her life. Presently she is writing several projects: a novel about the Maya set in the eighth century, a modern-day travelogue to Mayan regions, and a far-reaching chronology of her personal experiences aboard a Pleiadian Mothership. You may contact her by e-mail at spinyarn@aol.com.

Dharma Singh Khalsa, M.D., is president and medical director of the Alzheimer's Prevention Foundation (APF) in Tucson, Arizona. The APF is the world's leader in the integrated medical approach to the prevention and treatment of Alzheimer's disease. Dharma is also the author of *Brain Longevity, The Pain Cure,* and *Meditation as Medicine.* He can be reached by e-mail at Drdharma@aol.com.

Jill H. Lawrence is a journalist who specializes in topics from Angels to Zen. She hosts *Jill and Friends,* a live call-in talk show for Wisdom Radio (www.wisdomradio.com). She also serves as executive editor of *The Shifting Times Newsmagazine for Opening Minds.* She lives in Canton, Ohio.

Donna LeBlanc, M.Ed., D.A.P.A., is a psychotherapist, lecturer, author, and media personality residing in New York City. She has made regular appearances on the *Montel Williams Show, Queen Latifah, Good Day New York,* and many others. Her book, *You Can't Quit 'Til You Know What's Eating You,* published by Health Communications, has sold over 45,000 copies. Her upcoming book, *Busted: Breaking the Patterns That Screw*

Up Your Life, is based on her Four-Day Individual Personal Change Intensive. She has a national and international clientele. She lectures and provides workshops and seminars locally and around the country. She may be contacted at 212-799-8770, 877-633-6662 (877-63-DONNA), or on her Web site: www. donnaleblanc.com.

Mary Lennon is a singer-songwriter living in Los Angeles. She performs under the name Mare Lennon. Her debut CD, *Chasing Sacred,* was a Top Twelve DIY pick by *Performing Songwriter Magazine.* She has performed all over the world and recently was a featured performer on the Oxygen Tank Tour. Contact her by e-mail, marelennon@aol.com, or visit her Web site: http:// members@aol.com/marelennon.

Jill Lublin, owner of the public relations firm Promising Productions, has worked throughout the entertainment industry, with diverse businesses, and with national and international authors, seminar leaders, entrepreneurs, and nonprofit organizations. Her clients have been featured in major-market newspapers, magazines, and on ABC-, NBC-, and CBS-affiliated radio and television networks nationwide. Jill is the author of the upcoming book *Guerilla Publicity.* Contact her by e-mail at jill@planetlink.com.

Leslie Lynne is a human being, making a sincere attempt every day to be kind to herself and others. She has twenty years of experience in traditional family counseling and soul education. Leslie has taught in university, private, and workshop settings. She is cofounder of the WarmHeart Foundation and coordinates counseling, education, healer training, and curriculum development for the foundation. Leslie feels blessed and grateful to receive palpable divine love on a daily basis and enjoys sharing this love with everyone she touches in her work.

Jill V. Mangino is president of Circle 3 Productions, a media-communications company devoted to developing transformational programming for television, radio, and the Internet. She is a former freelance publicist, a segment producer for *Caucus: New Jersey* and *Families in Focus* (WNET-TV, NYC), and creator-associate producer of *Yogi Berra: Deja Vu All Over Again,* a PBS documentary that aired nationwide in August 1999. Jill was also the producer-host of *Positive Perspectives,* a radio talk show that aired on KWAI-AM in Honolulu, Hawaii. She can be reached via e-mail at circle3@aol.com.

Kathleen McGowan is a freelance writer, astrologer, and numerologist. She lives in Southern California with her husband and songwriter partner, Peter McGowan, and their two boys. Kathleen is the author of the numerology book *Star Stones.* She can be reached through the Web site for the McGowans' Celtic rock band, finnmaccool.com, or by e-mail at kdmcgowan@aol.com.

Alan Moore has been an environmental and peace activist for over thirty years, organizing campaigns for Common Cause, the Sierra Club, Solar Club, Solar Lobby, Public Citizen, and many other organizations. In 1993 he began his affair with butterflies and soon envisioned the Butterfly Gardeners Association. Its mission: to make the butterfly the symbol for a sustainable environment, world peace, and the conscious evolution of the human race. Recently he began working with Dr. Patch Adams to combine their lives' passions and dreams in what they will call Patch Adams Centers. The centers will promote environmental education, wildlife gardening for butterflies and hummingbirds, conservation, nonviolence reading programs, peace, volunteerism, community service, and organizing. Their latest campaign is to promote the butterfly as the "new Millennium Bug," representing personal and planetary transformation. Contact Alan and the Butterfly Gardeners Association by mail: 1563 Solano Ave., No. 477, Berkeley, CA 94707; phone: 510-528-7730; or e-mail: bflyspirit@aol.com.

Nancy E. Myer is an internationally recognized psychic detective. She has appeared on *Unsolved Mysteries, Sightings, The Other Side, Attitudes, 48 Hours, Paranormal Borderline,* and *Geraldo,* and contributed to the investigations of over 450 homicides in twenty-seven years. She has produced new information that was accurate 90 percent of the time. Articles about Nancy have appeared in numerous publications. She is the author of *Silent Witness: The True Story of a Psychic Detective.* Her work is mentioned in Time-Life's series *Mysteries of the Unknown, The Top Ten Psychics in America, Psychics, Psychic Detectives,* and *Who Killed My Daughter?* Nancy has a Web site at www.OnTVPittsburgh.com, "Nancy Myer's Psychic Tip of the Week." She works in Greensburg, Pennsylvania, where she does private readings, teaches meditation, and works on criminal cases. Her office number is 724-832-3951; address: P.O. Box 3015, Greensburg, PA 15601.

George R. Noory is a nationally renowned talk-show host for the ABC-affiliated station KTRS-AM in St. Louis, Missouri. His interviews have been recognized as some of the most provocative in the country. He is also a nine-year veteran of the United States Naval Reserve.

Cory Hunter Olson is a freelance writer and photographer, and a licensed massage therapist in Phoenix, Arizona. She is also the mother of four awesome kids. You can find her hiking in the mountains and desert near her home or by contacting information in Phoenix.

Josie RavenWing, M.A., M.F.C.C., is an internationally known pioneer in dance movement therapy and holistic healing, a psychotherapist, and a shamanic practitioner. She has studied and practiced multicultural healing methods, including shamanism and ceremonial healing, for over thirty years, integrating them with her Western training in psychology into a unique synthesis that she has taught in workshops nationally and abroad since 1983. She also takes people to Navajo land for extended spiritual retreats and on journeys to the famous healer Joao de Deus, and spiritual-healing ceremonies and centers of Brazil. Josie is a songwriter, poet, and the author of *Return of Spirit: A Woman's Call to Spiritual Action* and *A Season of Eagles,* and she has been widely interviewed by the media. Her poem "Song of the Journey" is included in Michael Harner's classic book on shamanism, *The Way of the Shaman*. To contact her write: P.O. Box 13162, Des Moines, IA 50310; or e-mail: JRaven Wing@aol.com.

Suzanne Rowe was born in Detroit, Michigan, on September 2, 1952, the oldest daughter of first-generation Italian and Lebanese parents. She has spent her life searching and seeking love, truth, and happiness. There have been sadness and mistakes made along the way, yet each experience has brought her closer to her goals and has increased her understanding of "what it's really all about." Suzanne firmly believes that what you give does come back! Presently she is in love with her husband, adores her beautiful adult son (another seeker!), and is blessed with wonderful family and friends. At age forty-seven she embarked on another career, and now enjoys writing, painting, and gardening, and finds the only thing lacking is enough time to do and see it all! She can be reached by e-mail at lunabella@aol.com.

Elizabeth Seely is writing her first book based on personal spiritual experiences. She lives in central Ohio with her two lovely little girls. She also works for an international trading company. She can be contacted by e-mail at elizseely@aol.com.

Deardra Shuler has worked in theater, music, television, and publishing, and has recently turned her attention to short story writing. She is a journalist and former managing editor of two New York City newspapers. Deardra writes freelance under her company name Writspirit and is an editor of the Web site entertainment magazine *New York Arts and Entertainment News*, which features all genres of events and venues in New York. She can be contacted through the Web site NYAEA.org.

Rosanne M. Siino has spent sixteen years in communications, with thirteen years in high-technology public relations for companies such as Netscape and Silicon Graphics. She currently serves as a strategic marketing and communications advisor to several Internet start-up companies in California's Silicon Valley. She can be reached by e-mail at rosanne@siino.org.

Jeremiah Sullivan is a marine biologist based out of San Diego, California. His expertise in shark behavior, particularly the human–shark interaction—how and why shark attacks occur—led to his invention and development of the steel mesh antishark suits in the early '80s. He has been involved in dozens of documentary films worldwide and continues to produce the state-of-the-art protective apparel for individuals who must work in hazardous situations in the sea.

James F. Twyman (a.k.a. the Peace Troubadour) has traveled the world performing the Peace Concert in areas affected by violence and war, including Bosnia, Iraq, Northern Ireland, Israel, and India. He is also the author of *Emissary of Light*.

Sally M. Veillette, currently living in Seattle, received a B.S. in electrical engineering from Brown University. For fourteen years she worked in marketing, advertising, and sales in high technology, most recently as vice president and general manager of a microelectronics manufacturing company. In 1993, after having been diagnosed with chronic fatigue syndrome, Sally lost her identity along with her energy. This started her on a journey to explore energy sources—those that affect the physical body as well as those that change the course of our business. Sally writes and speaks on these subjects and networks with leaders in the field. She has become a bridge between the spiritual community and the high-powered, high-pressured business world.

Doreen Virtue, Ph.D., holds three degrees in counseling psychology and works with the angelic realm. She is the author of *Divine Guidance, The Lightworker's Way,* and *Angel Therapy,* numerous audiotapes, and the Healing with the Angels oracle card deck. She has appeared on *Oprah,* CNN, and *The View,* and has been featured in *Redbook, Woman's Day,* and *Cosmopolitan,* among other publications. Doreen has successfully taught thousands of people around the globe how to connect with their angels. For more information call 800-654-5126, ext. 0, or visit Doreen's Web site, www.angeltherapy.com.

Lora Vivas is an educator who has worked with children of all ages. Her work with them includes meditation and visualization, as well as community service related to learning and curriculum in schools. It is her greatest desire to strengthen the connection between children and the world around them—and therefore the world within them. She has written a series of children's stories that relate the virtues of Deepak Chopra's *Seven Spiritual Laws for Parents* in child-friendly terms. She has lived in many splendid areas around the United States, and currently enjoys beautiful sunsets over the Rockies from her home near Boulder, Colorado. She can be reached by e-mail at blvivas@aol.com, or by phone at 303-447-5001, ext. 6120.

Judith Wright is the CSO (Chief Spiritual Officer) and, with her husband, Bob, cofounder of the School of Exceptional Living, a lifelong learning center devoted to developing human potential in growth and spiritual development with campuses in Chicago and Wisconsin. Since their "moment in midair," Judith and Bob are even more determined to make their vision of the possible a human reality for as many as they can. Judith is writing a book on the vision that came to her right after the incident, and Bob is writing a book on loving life. They would love to hear from or share with you via their Web site, www.exceptionalliving. com; or call 312-329-1200, or visit them at 445 East Ohio, Suite 260, Chicago, IL 60611.

George Wrigley is an ordained minister, wedding consultant, and DJ. He owns and operates Weddings by George and also writes, speaks regularly at churches in Phoenix and Tucson, Arizona, gives lectures, and conducts workshops. One of his hobbies and passions is building and flying airplanes. George can be reached by phone at 520-424-9680, or by e-mail at gwrigley@casagrande. com.

Arielle Ford has been a publicist for the past twenty years. She specializes in representing leaders in the fields of new thought, human potential, and mind-body medicine. Her clients have included Deepak Chopra, Debbie Ford, Jack Canfield, Mark Victor Hansen, Neale Donald Walsch, Gary Zukav, Wayne Dyer, Gregg Braden, and Marianne Williamson. She is the author of the book series *Hot Chocolate for the Mystical Soul*. *Magical Souvenirs* is her fifth book. She lives in La Jolla, California, with her husband, Brian, and two furry felines. You can reach her at fordgroup@aol.com; or fax her at 858-454-3319.

Plume books by
ARIELLE FORD

"Will challenge your beliefs, stretch your mind, and open your heart." —Jack Canfield, coauthor of *Chicken Soup for the Soul*